Ivan Moscovich's
MASTERMIND COLLECTION

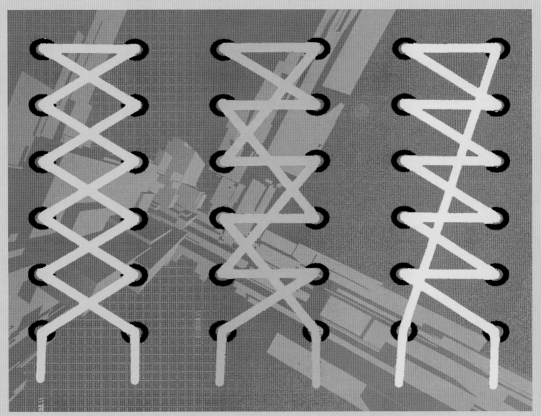

The Shoelace Problem
& Other Puzzles

STERLING PUBLISHING CO., INC.
New York

To Anitta, Hila, and Emilia, with love

Ivan Moscovich Mastermind Collection:
The Shoelace Problem & Other Puzzles was edited, designed, and typset by Imagine Puzzles Ltd.,
London (info@imaginepuzzles.com)

EDITORIAL DIRECTOR
Alison Moore
ASSISTANT EDITOR
David Popey
ART EDITOR
Keith Miller
CONSULTANT EDITOR
David Bodycombe
PROJECT MANAGER
Tamiko Rex
PUBLISHING DIRECTOR
Hal Robinson

Clipart: Nova Development Corporation

Library of Congress Cataloging-in-Publication Data Available

2 4 6 8 10 9 7 5 3 1

Published by Sterling Publishing Co., Inc.
387 Park Avenue South, New York, NY 10016
© 2004 by Ivan Moscovich
Distributed in Canada by Sterling Publishing
c/o Canadian Manda Group, 165 Dufferin Street,
Toronto, Ontario, Canada M6K 3H6
Distributed in Great Britain by Chrysalis Books Group PLC
The Chrysalis Building, Bramley Road, London W10 6SP, England
Distributed in Australia by Capricorn Link (Australia) Pty. Ltd.
P.O. Box 704, Windsor, NSW 2756, Australia

Sterling ISBN 1-4027-1669-9

Contents

Introduction

Ever since my high-school days I have loved puzzles and mathematical recreational problems. This love developed into a hobby when, by chance, some time in 1956, I encountered the first issue of *Scientific American* with Martin Gardner's mathematical games column. And for the past 50 years or so I have been designing and inventing teaching aids, puzzles, games, toys and hands-on science museum exhibits.

Recreational mathematics is mathematics with the emphasis on fun, but, of course, this definition is far too general. The popular fun and pedagogic aspects of recreational mathematics overlap considerably, and there is no clear boundary between recreational and "serious" mathematics. You don't have to be a mathematician to enjoy mathematics. It is just another language, the language of creative thinking and problem-solving, which will enrich your life, like it did and still does mine.

Many people seem convinced that it is possible to get along quite nicely without any mathematical knowledge. This is not so: Mathematics is the basis of all knowledge and the bearer of all high culture. It is never too late to start enjoying and learning the basics of math, which will furnish our all-too sluggish brains with solid mental exercise and provide us with a variety of pleasures to which we may be entirely unaccustomed.

In collecting and creating puzzles, I favour those that are more than just fun, preferring instead puzzles that offer opportunities for intellectual satisfaction and learning experiences, as well as provoking curiosity and creative thinking. To stress these criteria, I call my puzzles Thinkthings.

The *Mastermind Collection* series systematically covers a wide range of mathematical ideas, through a great variety of puzzles, games, problems, and much more, from the best classical puzzles taken from the history of mathematics to many entirely original ideas.

This book, *The Shoelace Problem & Other Puzzles*, contains many seemingly trivial puzzles and problems, such as the shoelace problem of the title. Behind this puzzle and many others, however, lie the serious principles of mathematics, waiting to be revealed to all who tackle them.

A great effort has been made to make all the puzzles understandable to everybody, though some of the solutions may be hard work. For this reason, the ideas are presented in a novel and highly esthetic visual form, making it easier to perceive the underlying mathematics.

More than ever before, I hope that these books will convey my enthusiasm for and fascination with mathematics and share these with the reader. They combine fun and entertainment with intellectual challenges, through which a great number of ideas, basic concepts common to art, science, and everyday life, can be enjoyed and understood.

Some of the games included are designed so that they can easily be made and played. The structure of many is such that they will excite the mind, suggest new ideas and insights, and pave the way for new modes of thought and creative expression.

Despite the diversity of topics, there is an underlying continuity in the topics included. Each individual Thinkthing can stand alone (even if it is, in fact, related to many others), so you can dip in at will without the frustration of cross-referencing.

I hope you will enjoy the *Mastermind Collection* series and Thinkthings as much as I have enjoyed creating them for you.

—Ivan Moscovich

The best puzzles are seldom what they seem. The solutions may demand that a common item be used in an unfamiliar way, that a conventional assumption be abandoned, or that components be assembled in an unusual arrangement. A direct, head-on approach often leads nowhere, while a lengthy detour can sometimes be the fastest route to a solution. When you are faced with a mental wall, the best approach is not to tunnel through it but to walk around it.

PIET HEIN (1905–1996)

Piet Hein, a Danish inventor, poet, and scientist, was a genius of wide-ranging interests. He popularized a new geometrical form, the "Superellipse" and the "Superegg," which helped solve the traffic problem of Sergel's Square in Stockholm more efficiently than either a rectangular or a circular layout.

He also invented a popular 3-D cube jigsaw puzzle, the Soma cube.

His poems, known as "Grooks," became famous when he operated as a resistance leader during World War II.

▲ HISTORY MYSTERY

This is a tribute to Ahmes, the scribe. Seven houses each have seven cats. Each cat kills seven mice. Each of the mice would have eaten seven ears of wheat. Each ear of wheat would have produced seven unit measures of flour. How many unit measures of flour were saved by the cats? (This puzzle dates from 1850 B.C, from the Ancient Egyptian Rhind Papyrus, written by Ahmes.)

ANSWER: **PAGE 98**

Taking fun as simply fun and earnestness in earnest shows how thoroughly thou none of the two discernest.
Piet Hein

Original thought is a straightforward process. It's easy enough when you know what to do. You simply combine in an appropriate dose the blatantly false and the patently true.
A "Grook" by Piet Hein

◀ POETRY CIRCLE

Can you decipher this Grook, as the short poems of Piet Hein (see above) are called?

ANSWER: **PAGE 98**

Your brain works even better then you might think. It is capable of making a virtually unlimited number of synaptic connections, each of which is a pattern of thought (the number of possible connections has been calculated, and the result is huge—1 followed by 60 million miles of zeros).

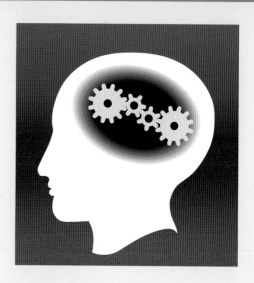

❋ Problem-solving: overcoming mental blocks

Learning means the ability to retain and retrieve information stored in the brain whenever it is needed.

About 100 billion contact points (synapses) create a vast network in our brains. Every experience we have changes these networks, and new patterns are established. A big brain needs a long time to grow, and to take in what it needs to know to survive in our intensely competitive culture. This implies a continuous lifelong education. On the other hand, there are sensitive periods in early childhood development when certain tasks must be learned.

In spite of the vast number of possible thoughts to think, thinking can be hard work, and there is a natural tendency to do as little of it as possible.

This tendency is seen in the hit-and-run approach many take to problem-solving: They pick the first solution that comes to mind and run with it.

Such an approach generally fails to take into account the full range of possible solutions. People can become trapped in their own preconceptions, and information that might solve the problem is not neglected so much as simply not perceived. Problem-solving always works best with the fewest self-imposed blinders.

The greater the choice of creative concepts, the better chance there is of finding an answer. If your first idea fails to solve the problem, try another. It is important to avoid the mental walls known as conceptual blocks, which can

shield us from even the simplest and most obvious answer.

Sometimes the conceptual block is of one's own creation, while others stem from incomplete information, emphasis on the wrong detail, or deliberately misleading directions. Inventors of puzzles and magic tricks exploit such conceptual blocks in order to lead suggestible minds up blind alleys.

But in spite of the universal tendency to suffer from mental blocks, most people at one time or another do use their brain to full capacity and tackle a problem of bewildering complexity, penetrate to its core, and extract an insight of startling simplicity and elegance that solves the problem at a stroke.

◀ NO EYE DEAR

There was a man who didn't have eyes. He went to the woods to view the skies. He saw a tree with apples on it. He didn't take apples off it, yet he didn't leave apples on it.

How could that be?

ANSWER: PAGE 98

▶ ST. IVES RIDDLE

Ahmes's puzzle on page 7 has inspired many variations, among them the St. Ives riddle. Leonardo of Pisa (Fibonacci) published the rhyme in 1202 in his Liber Abaci. *The rhyme is as follows:*

"As I was going to St. Ives, I met a man with seven wives. Every wife had seven sacks. Every sack had seven cats. Every cat had seven kits. Kits, cats, sacks, and wives. How many were going to St. Ives?"

ANSWER: PAGE 98

We are all potentially creative; we just don't think creatively most of the time. Seeing in new ways involves seeing the commonplace with new perceptions, transforming the familiar to the strange, and the strange to the familiar.

When did you smile for the first time?

You can probably remember the last time you smiled, but what about the first time?

Until now it was believed that babies first smile only about five or six weeks after birth, when they learn expressions by copying their mothers. New ultrasound scanning machines have revealed, however, that unborn children can smile in the womb, providing convincing high-quality photos of smiling fetuses. Does this indicate that it is never too early to provide the right experiences, such as puzzles?

✳ Creativity and intelligence?

Creativity is difficult to define. It is more than just the process by which new ideas are generated. Creativity is really a different way of thinking, one that is less preoccupied with details than with fundamental relationships. It is less concerned with facts and numbers than it is with arrangements and connections. And, indeed, the more connections a creative mind can make, the more paths that are open for finding a unique and satisfying answer to a problem.

The British psychologist Edward de Bono calls this mind-set "lateral thinking," and it is commonly found not only in pioneering scientific minds but also in artists and other visionaries. Yet these people are not endowed with any special gift: For the first five years of life, every child is a creative thinker, but we acquire mental blocks as we get

older that obscure the essence of problems and lead us away from even obvious solutions.

Most of us grew up with a concept of intelligence that is driven by tests: The person who can answer the most questions is thought to be the most intelligent. But imagining that intelligence can be boiled down to a single number in this way—the IQ—is now an obsolete notion.

Another flaw in early attitudes was the idea that intelligence is fixed at birth. Much recent research has shown that IQ scores can be significantly raised through appropriate training. The American researcher Bernard Devlin concluded that genes account for no more than 48 percent of IQ; the other 52 percent is the function of prenatal care, environment, and education.

"The really valuable thing is intuition," said Einstein. In recent years, intuition has increasingly been recognized as a natural mental faculty, a key element in discovery, problem-solving, and decision-making, a generator of creative ideas and a revealer of truth. We are all intuitive, and we can all be more intuitive. There is a growing conviction that perhaps we ought to trust the hunches, vague feelings, premonitions, and inarticulate signals that we usually ignore.

So if you find yourself having difficulty with some of these puzzles, don't worry that you are not "smart" enough to do them. It is all a matter of freeing up your latent creativity. With the proper mind-set, anyone can do these puzzles.

And if you find the puzzles easy, congratulations!

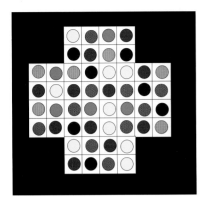

◀ WINDOW BOX

Through this cross-shaped window in a square on the left, we can see a part of the colored pattern below.

How long will it take you to position the square in its proper place, overlapping the colors on the pattern of dots?

Half a minute, two minutes, or more?

ANSWER: PAGE 98

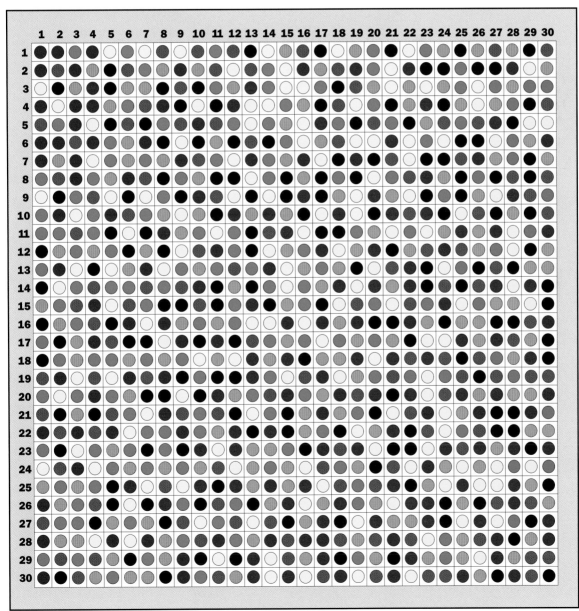

Some of the simplest codes are the most effective. Caesar used a code where a strip of letters was wound around a stick; the message could be read only if your stick was the right diameter. Even when you're presented with something familiar, it can take you a surprisingly long time to decipher the meaning.

▲ **MYSTERY SIGNS 1**

Can you decipher the hidden message above?

ANSWER: PAGE 98

▲ MYSTERY SIGNS 2

Can you find the missing sign here?

ANSWER: PAGE 98

Vaudeville acts turned a simple activity such as paper-folding and tearing into a performance art form. On these pages, we've provided you with your own chance to let rip!

PAPER VIEW 1 ▶

A square piece of paper is folded in half and half again as shown on the right.

   Differently shaped holes are cut through the folded piece as shown in the examples below.

   When the pieces are unfolded, select the correct pattern obtained from the four given colored alternatives.

ANSWER: PAGE 98

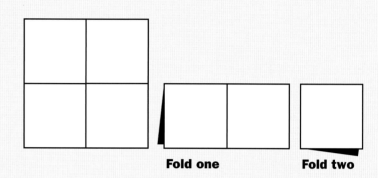

Fold one   **Fold two**

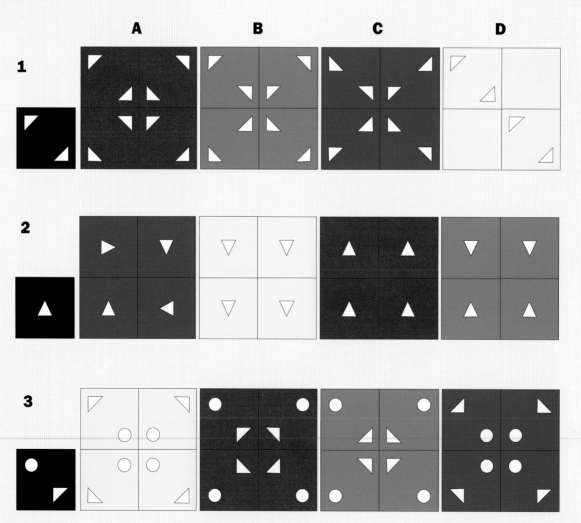

A   B   C   D

◀ **PAPER VIEW 2**

This time a rectangular piece of paper is folded, as shown on the left.

Again, differently shaped holes are cut through the folded piece as shown in the examples.

The pieces are then unfolded. Can you select the correct pattern obtained from the three given colored alternatives?

ANSWER: PAGE *98*

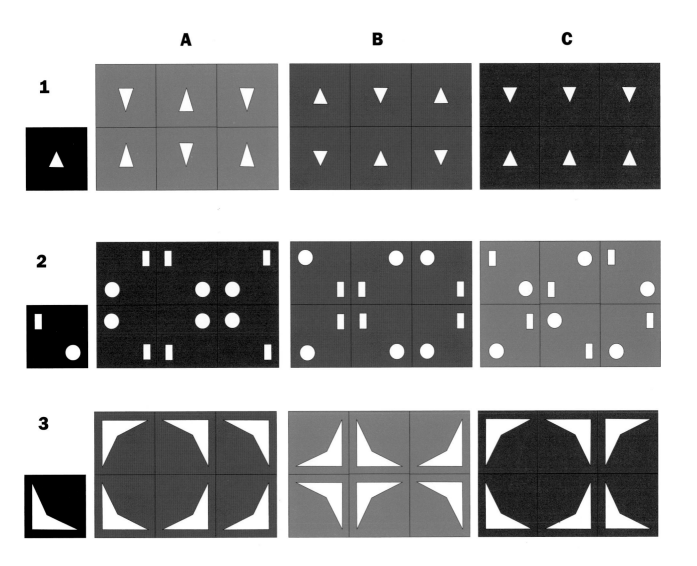

It's recently been discovered that bees from the same hive fly in perfectly straight lines but in different directions. This way, they don't compete with each other for food. See if you can make a beeline to the correct answers here.

DID YOU KNOW?

A typical graphic pencil could draw a single, unbroken line over 30 miles (50 km) long.

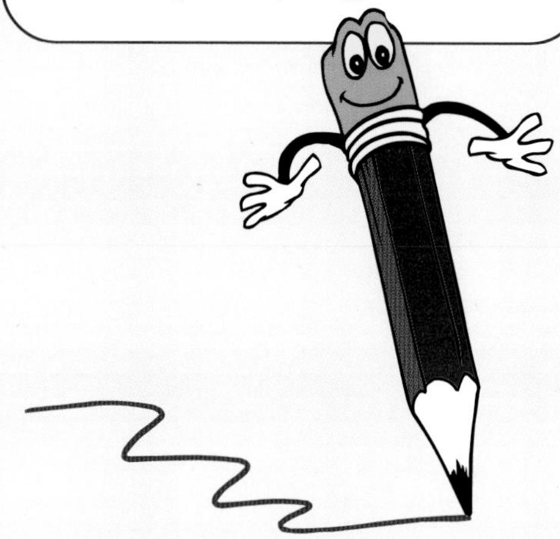

▼ SWEET SIXTEEN

Six straight lines are needed to create a continuous line through a square of 16 points, as shown below.

Puzzle 1 *Can you find any of the other 13 possible solutions?*

Puzzle 2 *How many solutions can you find that have the smallest number of intersections between the lines?*

Puzzle 3 *How many solutions can you find that form symmetrical patterns?*

ANSWER: PAGE 99

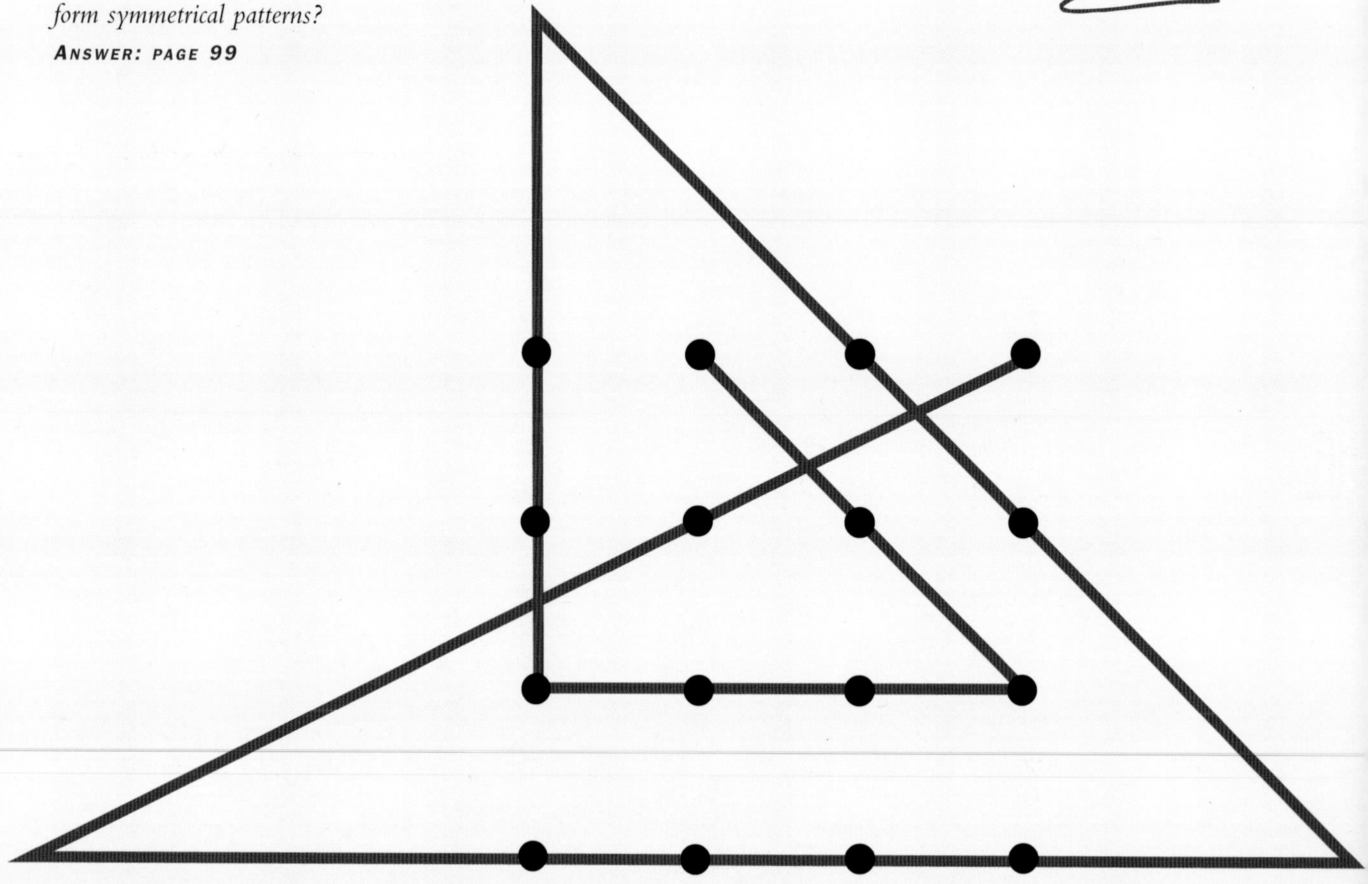

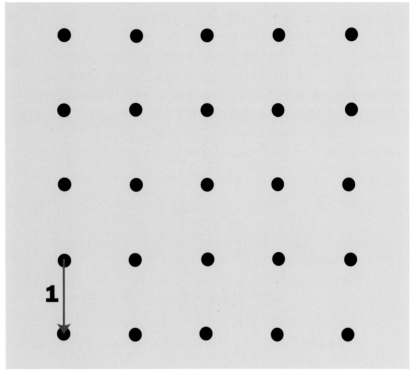

▶ TWENTY-FIVE SENSE

How many continuous straight line connections (up-down, left-right) can you make between two nearest points without crossing your path, starting from the point shown? Points may be reused.

ANSWER: PAGE 100

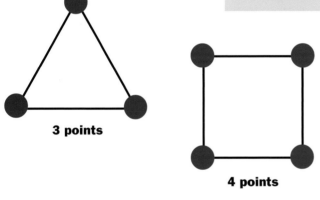

3 points

4 points

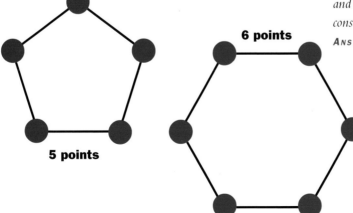

5 points

6 points

◀ ALL THE RIGHT CONNECTIONS

Given a number of points in the two-dimensional plane, how many different ways are there to join them up?

There is only one way of joining three points with a continuous series of straight lines ending at the starting point.

How many ways can you find for four, five, and six points? Rotations and reflections are not considered to be different.

ANSWER: PAGE 100

Difficult problems involving arrangements of "n" points on straight lines—so that exactly "k" points will be on each line—are often known as "tree-planting" or "orchard" problems. Usually the object is to maximize the number of lines "r." Curiously enough, the problem has not yet been solved, even for cases of k = 3 and k = 4, and a breakthrough is awaited.

? DID YOU KNOW?

The very first reference to tree-planting problems was in a book by John Jackson, published in 1821.

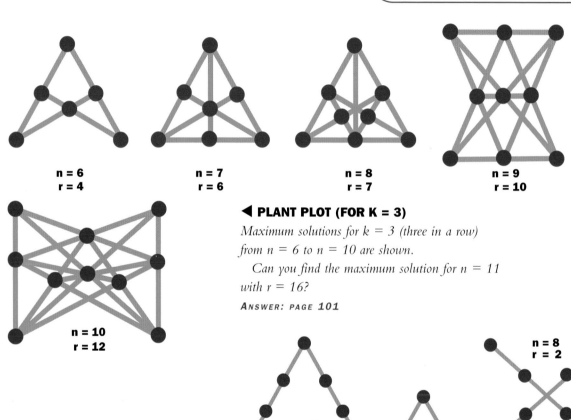

n = 6
r = 4

n = 7
r = 6

n = 8
r = 7

n = 9
r = 10

n = 10
r = 12

◀ PLANT PLOT (FOR K = 3)

Maximum solutions for k = 3 (three in a row) from n = 6 to n = 10 are shown.

Can you find the maximum solution for n = 11 with r = 16?

ANSWER: PAGE 101

▶ PLANT PLOT (FOR K = 4)

When k = 4 the problem becomes even more difficult. Maximum solutions for k = 4 (four in a row) from n = 7 to n = 12 are shown.

Can you find the maximum solution for n = 13 with r = 9?

ANSWER: PAGE 101

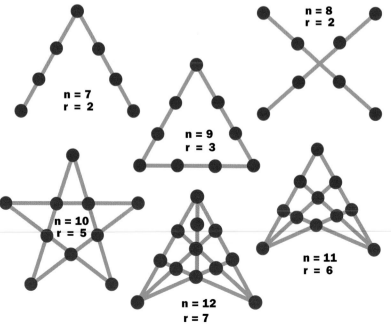

n = 7
r = 2

n = 8
r = 2

n = 9
r = 3

n = 10
r = 5

n = 11
r = 6

n = 12
r = 7

▲ TREE-MENDOUS

Place red counters on the white circles, so you have three red counters on every straight line.

How many red counters will you need altogether?

ANSWER: PAGE 101

Nonograms (or paint by numbers puzzles) are popular puzzles found in many newspapers and magazines in which logical series of numbers can be used to deduce simple pictures. Here we present two other forms of hiding pictures in logical ways.

▼ PICTURE STRIP

A picture is hidden in the pattern. Can you discover the secret principle on which the pattern was hidden, and rediscover the picture?

ANSWER: PAGE **102**

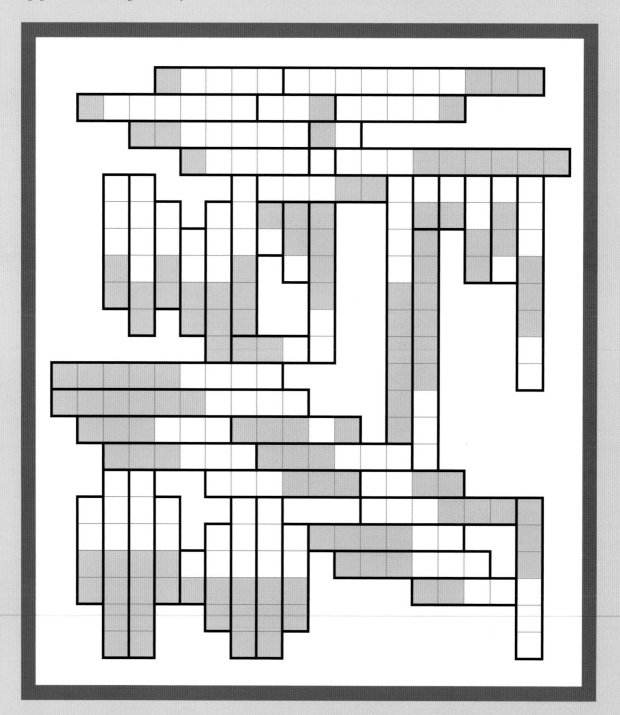

◀ **LOOK OUT!**

A picture is scrambled in this square-tiles color pattern at left.

Can you discover the secret principle on which the pattern was scrambled, and reconstruct it by sliding the rows and columns of tiles?

What does the scrambled picture reveal?

ANSWER: PAGE 103

Recreational math puzzles, particularly those that could be posed without the need for expensive diagrams, were popular in newspapers and journals from the late 19th century. See how you get on with these puzzles in the 21st century.

◄ FLASHPOINT

The bridge above will collapse in exactly 17 minutes. The four hikers must cross the bridge in that time in pitch darkness. They have only one flashlight between them, which is needed for each crossing.

A maximum of two people can cross the bridge at one time carrying the flashlight, which must be returned by hand after each crossing.

Each hiker walks at a different speed: One takes 1 minute to cross, another takes 2 minutes, and the others take 5 and 10 minutes respectively. Each pair crosses the bridge at the rate of the slower hiker's pace (so, for example, hiker 1 crossing with hiker 3 will cross the bridge in 5 minutes).

No tricks are allowed: The flashlight cannot be thrown back, no hiker is allowed to carry another, etc.

There are two possible solutions. Can you find either of them?

ANSWER: PAGE **104**

▶ SWEEEET

A piece of cake and a sundae cost two and a half dollars between them, but the cake costs a dollar more than the sundae.

How much does each cost?

ANSWER: PAGE 104

◀ SNAIL'S PACE

A little snail climbed up a window 90 units high. If every day it climbed up 11 units, and every night it dropped back 7 units, how many days without a stop did the little snail take to reach the top?

ANSWER: PAGE 104

As you'll see here, circles within circles can lead to unexpected answers. But perhaps the biggest surprise is how circles can be stacked into a neat triangle. (Here's a hint—the solution involves a square!)

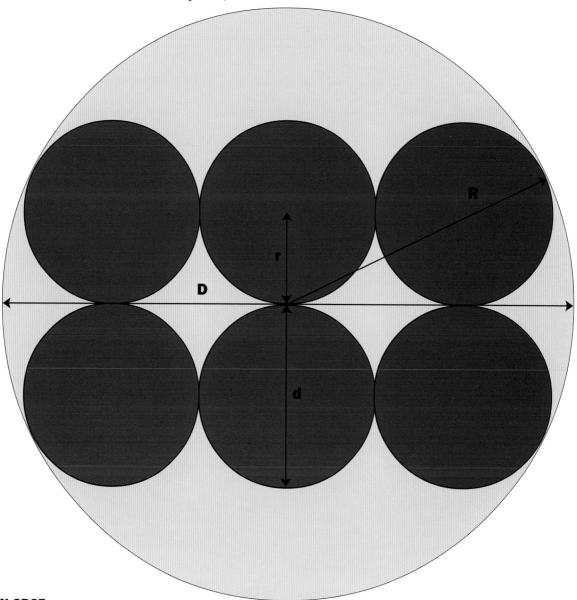

▲ SIX SPOT

On both halves of the diameter of the large circle, three identical smaller circles are inscribed as shown.

Can you work out the ratio of the radius of the big circle in terms of the diameter of one of the small circles?

ANSWER: PAGE 104

▼ TRICKY TRIANGLE

With nothing more than the number 1 and the notion of adding, and with the creative leap to represent numbers as geometrical patterns such as triangles, ancient Greek mathematicians found startling patterns, proofs, and shortcuts.

What is the result of adding up all the natural numbers from 1 to 17, without the need to add up each and every one?

Finding the right shortcut will give you the 17th triangular number, shown below. What will the 40th triangular number be?

ANSWER: PAGE **105**

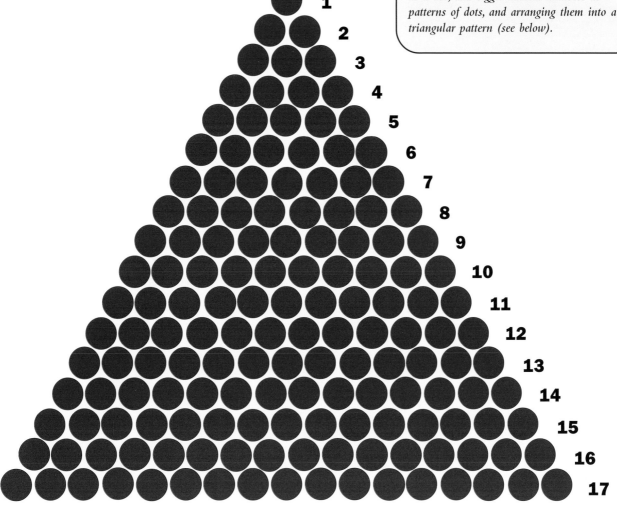

Projective geometry has its origins in the works of the Renaissance artists, who revived the ancient Greek doctrine that the essence of nature is mathematical law. Renaissance painters struggled for over 100 years to find a mathematical scheme to enable them to depict the three-dimensional world on a two-dimensional canvas. Finally they succeeded.

✳ Projective geometry

The development of projective and analytical geometry led mathematicians to the possibility of studying the geometry of spaces with more than three dimensions.

Our eyes present a distorted view of the world. For example, the parallel tracks of a railroad should never meet, but rails in the distance do look as if they come to a point. Large objects looks small when they are far off, and distance can make two objects of equal size appear to be on radically different scales. The reverse is true as well: A thumb can obscure the largest galaxy.

Even though human perception of scale is a given, it was only during the Renaissance that painters solved the problem of representing the perspective of a three-dimensional space on a two-dimensional plane. That solution, called projection, created not only a breakthrough in art but also a

new type of geometry—a form of mathematics that closely approaches the world of illusion.

Projective geometry studies what happens to shapes when they are distorted in special ways. Although the results can be startling, projective transformations preserve many of the geometric properties of the objects being projected. It is this factor that enables three-dimensional objects to be recognizable in their two-dimensional form.

These days we come into contact with the uses of projective geometry every day. Maps are projections, while photographs are images of projections, as are many mechanical and architectural drawings. And video games in realistic 3-D are possible only because sophisticated computer programs can calculate the projection of imaginary three-dimensional objects.

▶ BACK IN THE FOLD

On the right are unfolded cubes with designs on their faces (A–E). Next to each are four isometric drawings of cubes. The object in each case is to match up each isometric cube with the correct unfolded cube.

ANSWER: PAGE 105

❓ DID YOU KNOW?

When held at arm's length, a garden pea is large enough to cover the moon.

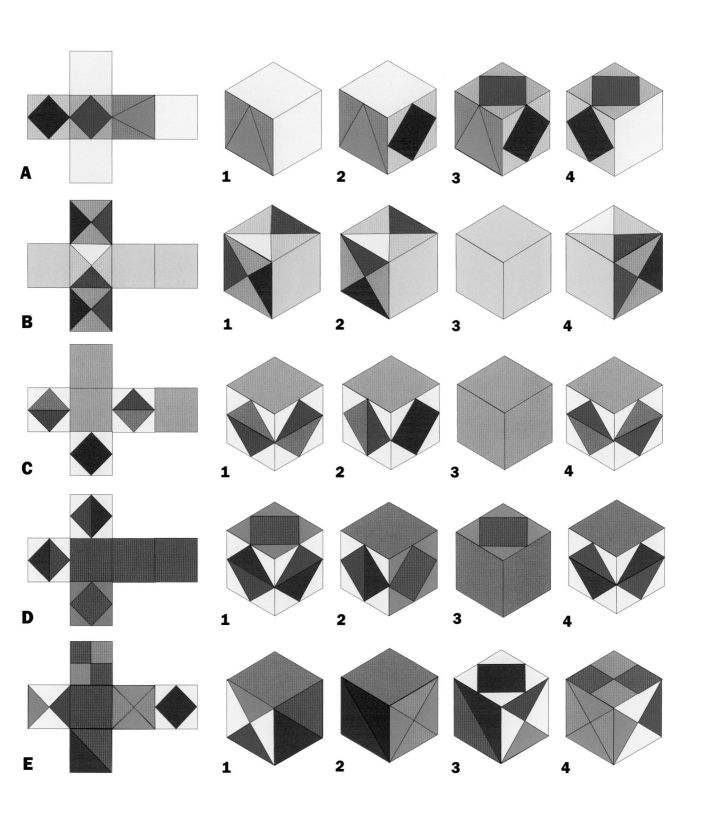

A

1 2 3 4

B

1 2 3 4

C

1 2 3 4

D

1 2 3 4

E

1 2 3 4

Sit yourself down and prepare to tackle some challenging puzzles on these pages. If you need something to occupy your hands, there's a blanket waiting to be unpicked opposite.

▼ SEATING ARRANGEMENT

In how many different ways can you seat men and women in a row of four chairs so that no two women sit next to each other?

Can you come to an interesting conclusion generalizing this problem for "n" number of chairs and work out the answers for any number of chairs?

ANSWER: PAGE **105**

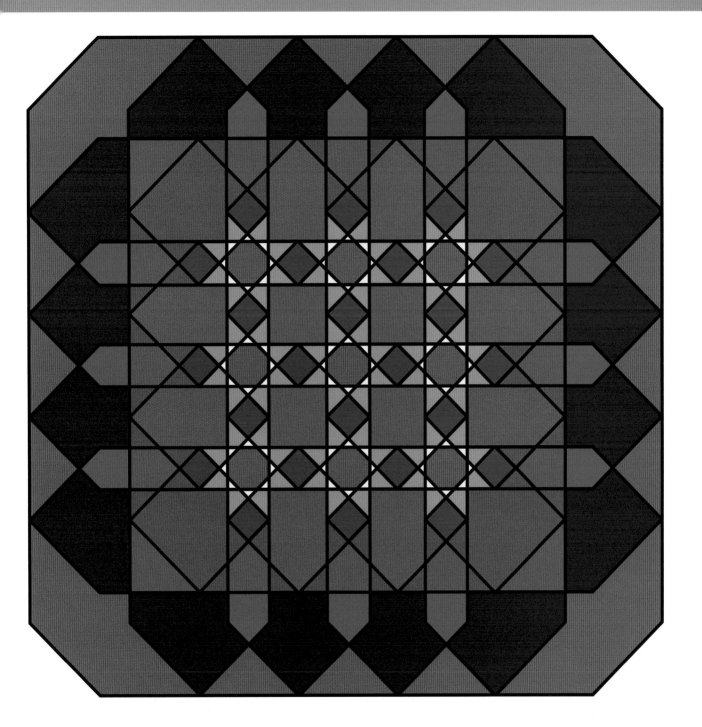

▲ BLANKET COVERAGE

This intricate tessellation consisting of triangles, squares, pentagons, hexagons, heptagons, and octagons was created from one single element. Can you determine what this is and how the pattern was created?

ANSWER: PAGE 105

Suppose you encoded a piece of text as A = 1, B = 2, C = 3, etc. For any finite text you choose, even a whole book, the corresponding code numbers can be found in the digits of π because it is an infinitely long nonrepeating sequence. The sequences herein are rather shorter.

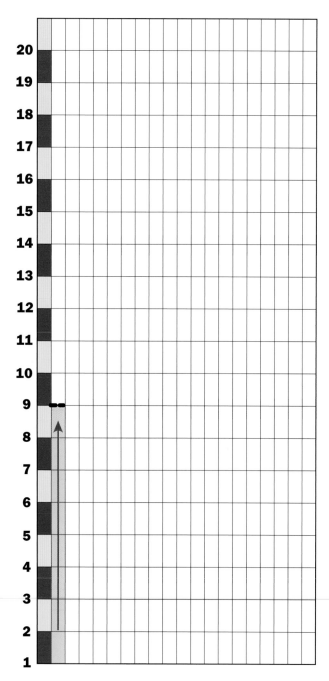

◀ AN UP AND DOWN CAREER

In this 20-floor building there is only one strange elevator, which has just two buttons: one up and the other down. The up button takes you up eight floors (or doesn't move at all if there are not eight floors available), and the down button takes you down 11 floors (or doesn't move if there are not 11 floors available).

Is it possible to get from the ground to any floor by taking the elevator?

How many times will the maintenance man have to push the buttons to get from the ground to all the other floors and in what sequence will he visit the floors?

ANSWER: PAGE *106*

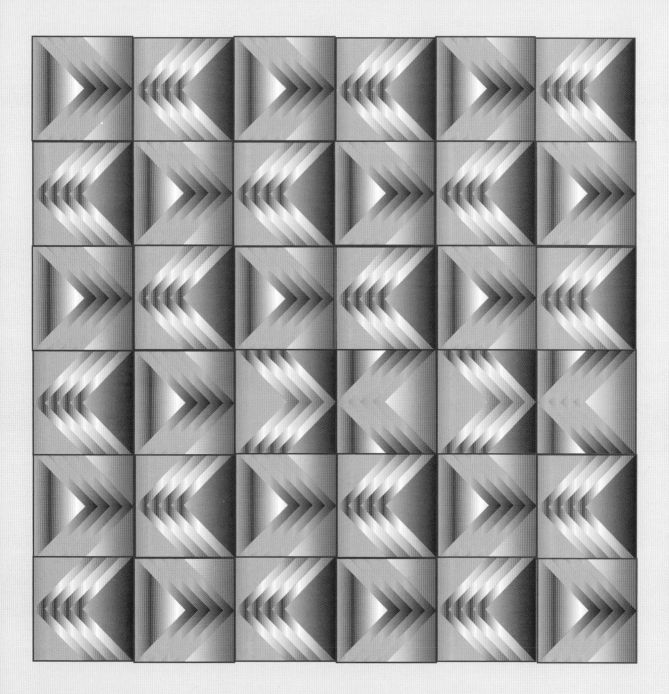

▲ **RIGHT THIS WAY**

The plan was to lay the tiles in rows, with every other tile pointing in the opposite direction. From which tile did the sequence go wrong?

ANSWER: PAGE 107

Getting lost isn't so easy these days, thanks to technology. GPS systems can pinpoint your position to an incredible degree of certainty. Just make sure the batteries don't run out.

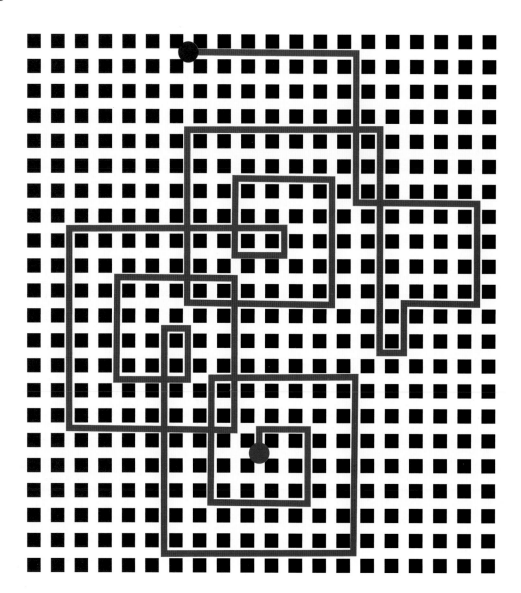

▲ INSIDE MOLE

The mole starts from the red point, with the red line showing its path until its end at the blue point.

Can you work out the logic of its path until the point at which it changed the rule? At which point did this happen?

ANSWER: PAGE 107

▼ PATHFINDER

Different shortest paths leading from the top left to bottom right points along the square grids of 2-by-2 and 3-by-3 squares are shown.

Can you work out how many different shortest paths there are along the grids of a 4-by-4 square? You must not cross the dotted line on your route.

ANSWER: PAGE 107

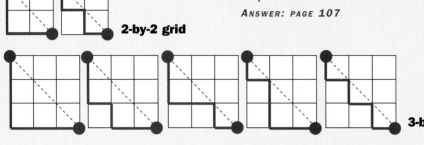

2-by-2 grid

3-by-3 grid

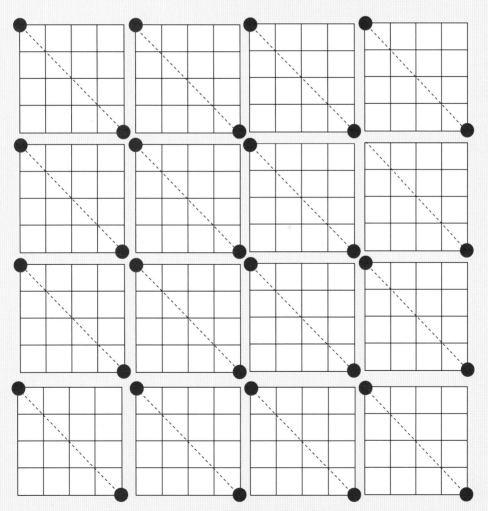

4-by-4 grid

In Switzerland, there exists an "ideas shop" where you pay some money and the staff will try to make some practical suggestions to solve any problem you have. It'll be much cheaper if you try to solve these problems by yourself.

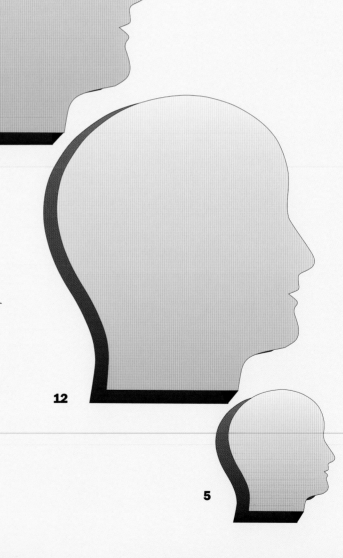

13

12

5

▶ GOLDEN JUBILEE

The king has ordered a golden plaque of his profile for a commemorative celebration.

He was presented with three plaques, each one of identical thickness and proportions but of different sizes.

The width at the neck was 13, 12, and 5 units respectively.

Which should he choose to maximize the amount of gold used: the two smaller heads or the big head only?

ANSWER: PAGE 108

◀ **WHO IS A MILLIONAIRE?**

Three of these people are celebrating their millionth birthdays. One has lived for a million hours, the other a million minutes, and the third a million seconds. Can you identify their approximate ages? Which person is the odd one out?

ANSWER: PAGE 108

▶ **FIRE DRILL**

At a recent fire a fireman stood on the middle rung of a ladder directing water into the burning building. As the smoke diminished, he stepped up three rungs and continued his work from that point.

A sudden flare-up forced him to descend five rungs. Later he climbed up seven rungs and worked there until the fire was out.

Then he climbed the six remaining rungs and entered the building.

How many rungs were there on the ladder?

ANSWER: PAGE 108

These two puzzles demonstrate that even when the amount of information is very limited, the answer can be surprisingly specific.

▶ ID PARADE

Mac was exactly in the middle of the lineup according to the heights of the inmates.

His jailmate Nick was higher up in the 13th position, and another, Jim, was even higher, at the 20th position.

How many inmates took part in the lineup given that each inmate was different in height?

ANSWER: PAGE **109**

▶ TRICKY TELEPATHY

Pick any two-digit number, add up its two digits, then subtract that sum from your chosen number.

On the right is the table of the first 100 numbers, including all the two-digit numbers, with each number accompanied by a color.

Look up the number that resulted from your subtraction.

No matter what your initial number was, the crystal ball says it will be accompanied by a blue color code, either light blue or dark blue.

Can you explain the "magic"?

ANSWER: PAGE **109**

0	1	2	3	4	5
6	7	8	9	10	11
12	13	14	15	16	17
18	19	20	21	22	23
24	25	26	27	28	29
30	31	32	33	34	35
36	37	38	39	40	41
42	43	44	45	46	47
48	49	50	51	52	53
54	55	56	57	58	59
60	61	62	63	64	65
66	67	68	69	70	71
72	73	74	75	76	77
78	79	80	81	82	83
84	85	86	87	88	89
90	91	92	93	94	95
96	97	98	99		

Estimating angles is a useful skill no matter whether you're parking the car or sinking a pool ball. How well can you judge angles using just your eyes?

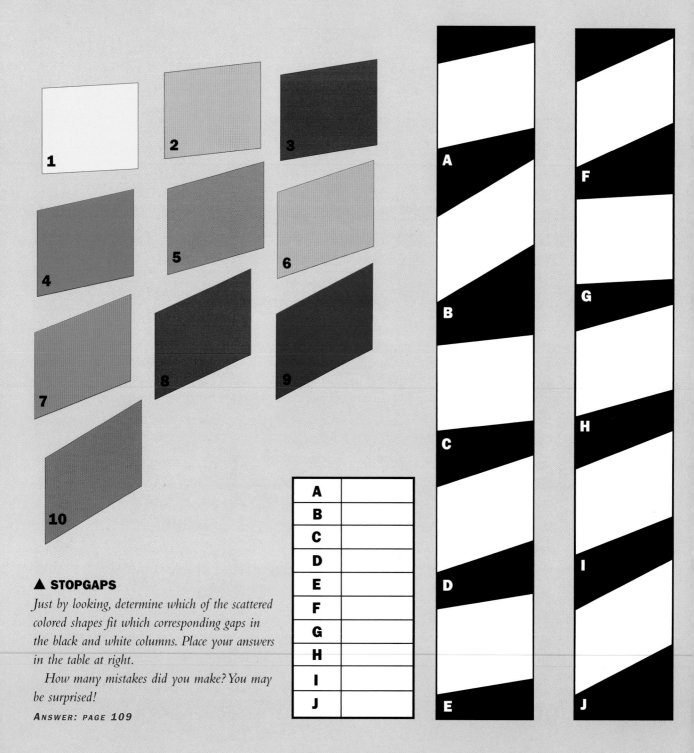

▲ **STOPGAPS**

Just by looking, determine which of the scattered colored shapes fit which corresponding gaps in the black and white columns. Place your answers in the table at right.

How many mistakes did you make? You may be surprised!

ANSWER: PAGE 109

A	
B	
C	
D	
E	
F	
G	
H	
I	
J	

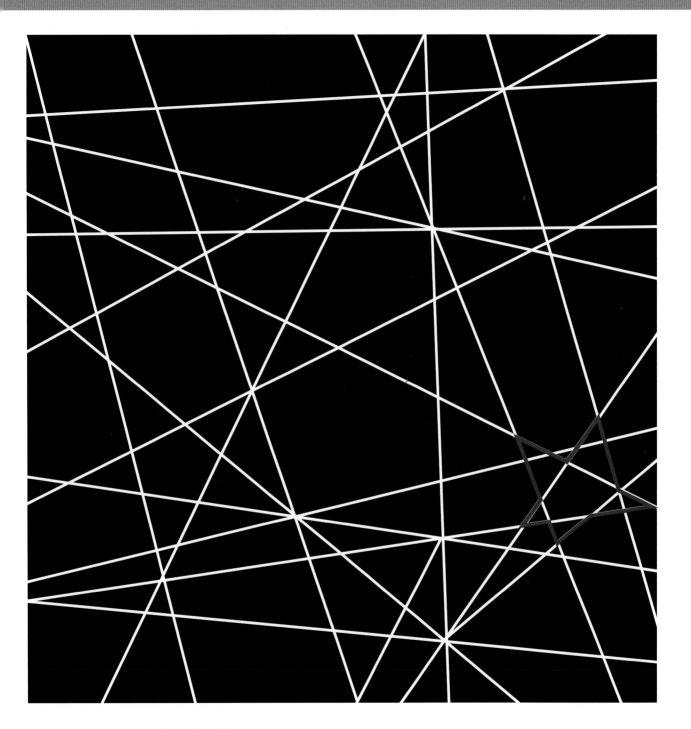

▲ FIVE STAR

These lines are "describing" (producing) polygons. How many different irregular pentagonal stars, like the one shown in red, can you find in the pattern of lines?

ANSWER: PAGE *110*

Matchsticks are among the cheapest and simplest objects on which to base geometrical puzzle problems. Many volumes have been devoted to matchstick problems, some of which have become classics.

1.

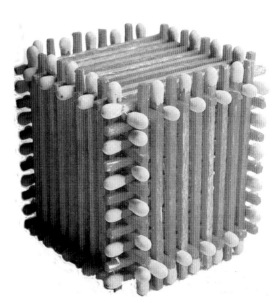

Classic matchstick problems

1. Match cube—Can you create a solid cube from matchsticks, without using glue or any other means with which to join them?
2. 15 matchsticks—Can you lift 15 matchsticks with one single match?
3. Match bridge—Can you create a rigid, free-standing bridge from 18 matchsticks, again without using glue or any other means to join them? (Hint: Do it lying on its side then stand it up.)

2.

3.

? DID YOU KNOW?

The first known description of a matchstick puzzle was published as long ago as 1858.

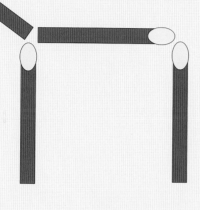

▼ DEER, OH DEER!

The magician Mel Stover challenged me with this puzzle one day over breakfast at one of Martin Gardner's Gatherings in Atlanta.

Change only one single matchstick to let the Bambi look in another direction without changing its shape in any way.

Reflections and rotations are allowed. It took me quite a while to find the solution.

ANSWER: PAGE 110

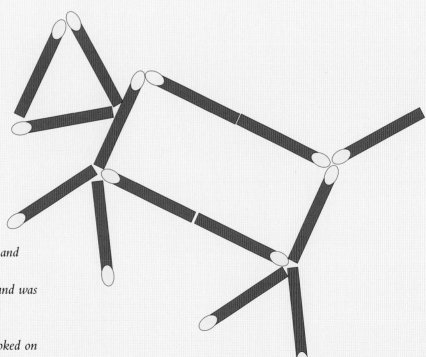

▶ DOGGED DETERMINATION

This playful dog was not careful enough and was hit by an automobile.

Fortunately, he wasn't too badly hurt and was taken to a vet.

By changing the positions of only two matchsticks, can you visualize how he looked on the vet's table?

ANSWER: PAGE 110

Matchsticks were invented by a chemist called John Walker in 1827. Funnily enough, it was completely accidental. He dipped a wooden stick into a material he was perfecting for shotguns, and it burst into flames when he scraped the stick on the stone floor to clean it.

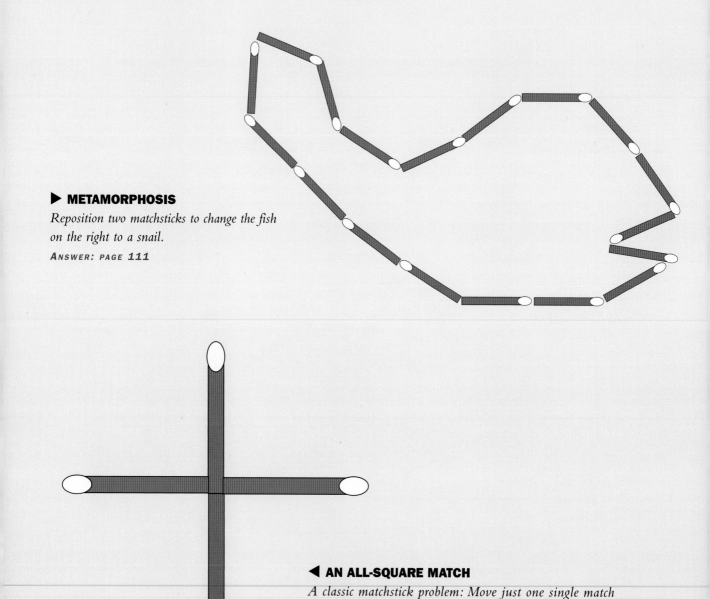

▶ METAMORPHOSIS

Reposition two matchsticks to change the fish on the right to a snail.

ANSWER: PAGE 111

◀ AN ALL-SQUARE MATCH

A classic matchstick problem: Move just one single match to create a geometric square.

ANSWER: PAGE 111

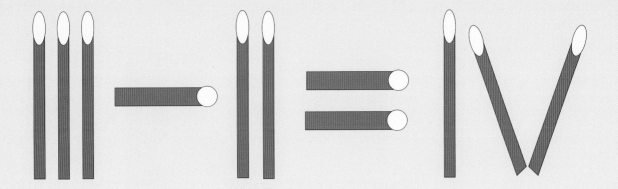

▲ EVERYTHING'S EQUAL

Can you change only one matchstick to get the correct equation? Can you find a second solution?

ANSWER: PAGE 111

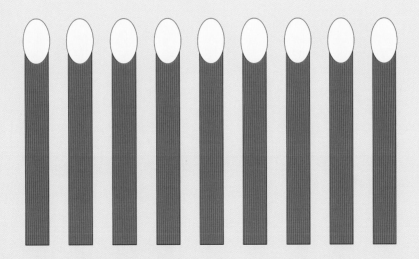

▲ MATCH PLAY

Can you make ten from only nine matches?

ANSWER: PAGE 111

Illustrators such as Kit Williams and Mike Wilks have used objects and animals hidden within seemingly normal illustrations to create amazingly subtle puzzles. In this puzzle, the art style is more akin to Mondrian!

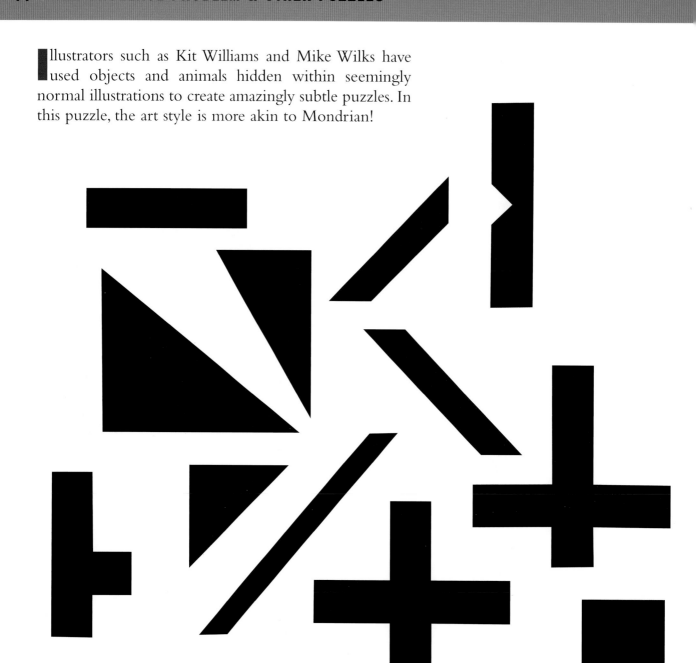

▲ ARTY-CRAFTY

How long will it take you to find the shapes above in the pattern on the right?

The shapes may overlap more than one colored region, but they can be found in the same size and the same orientations as above.

ANSWER: PAGE 112

These puzzles demonstrate two key benefits of perception: to simplify situations and identify patterns within
confusing extraneous information.

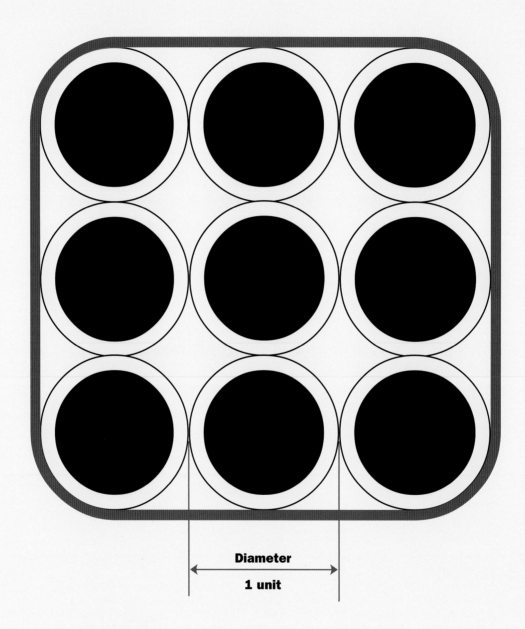

Diameter

1 unit

▲ **PIPE BAND**

Nine pipes are tied tightly together by a red metal band.
How long is the band?

ANSWER: PAGE 113

▼ COVERT CUBES

How many complete skeleton 3-D rectangular prisms can you see in this geometric design? One example is highlighted here in red.

ANSWER: PAGE 113

Tracers are used in items as diverse as ammunition and barium meals to help the eye follow an otherwise unseen path. All you'll need to trace these paths is a pencil, however.

◀ TRACK AND TRACE

Can the figures on this page be traced without lifting your pencil? No part of the figures, except for intersection points, should be traced more than once.

ANSWER: PAGE 114

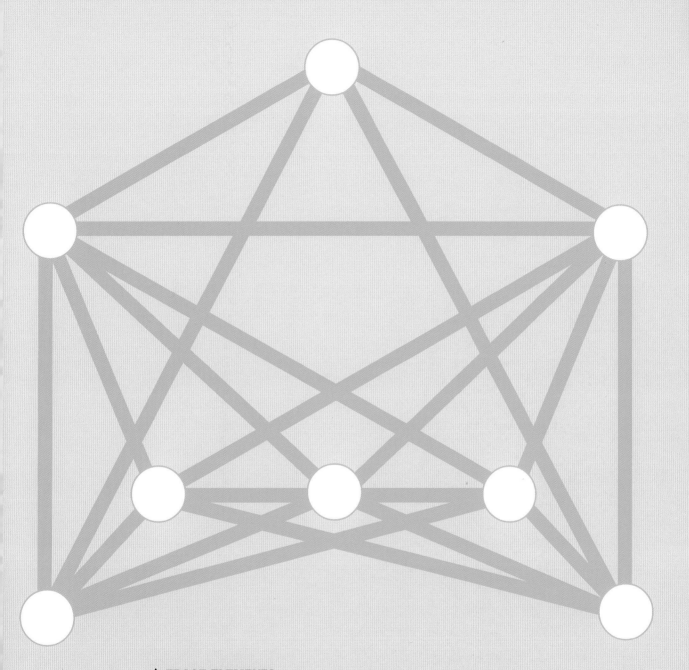

▲ TRACE ELEMENTS

Imagine putting your pencil on a white circle somewhere in this pattern. Try to trace the whole pattern along the green lines without taking your pencil off the paper, and without leaving any lines untraced. The lines you trace may cross, but they are not allowed to be retraced.

Can you trace the whole pattern, and, if so, under what conditions?

ANSWER: PAGE 114

▼ RETURN JOURNEYS

Just by looking, how many of the patterns on these pages do you think you could draw without raising your pencil or retracing a line?

ANSWER: PAGE 115

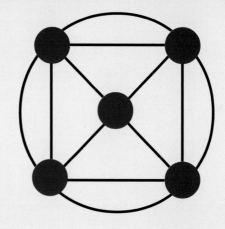

1

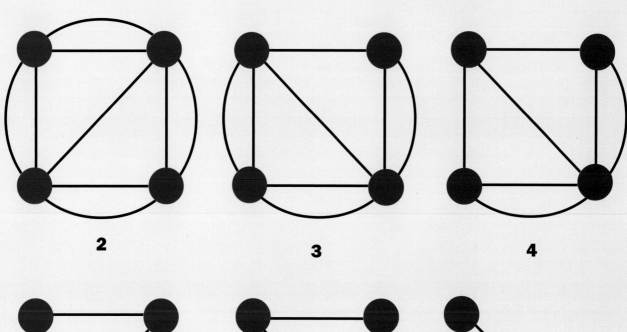

2   **3**   **4**

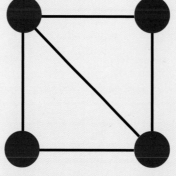

5   **6**   **7**

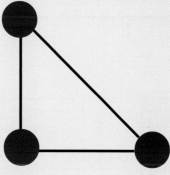

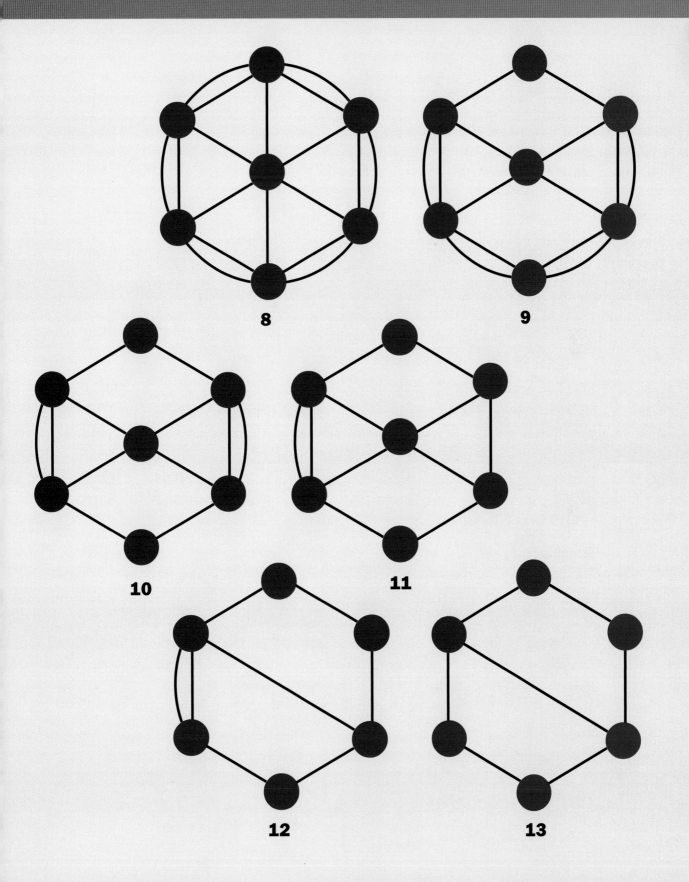

According to legend, the basalt columns of the Giant's Causeway in Northern Ireland are ancient steppingstones used by giants to cross the channel between Ireland and Scotland. The steppingstones here are rather more modest.

▼ FOUR-WAY MAZE

Start at one of the four arrows. Move from square to square horizontally or vertically according to this sequence:
yellow–red–green–blue.

Repeat this sequence until you reach the center, avoiding black squares. The center square may be reached from any color square. Which arrow leads to the shortest route to the center?

ANSWER: PAGE 115

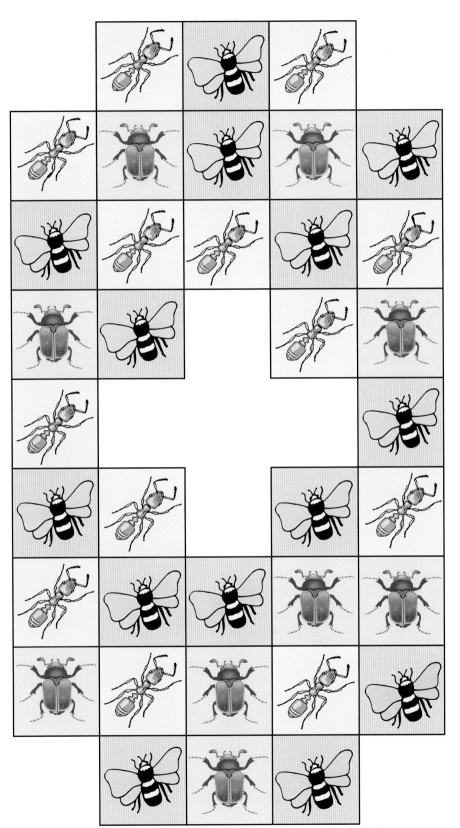

◄ INSECT-A-SIDE

How many of these insect cells can you visit without going through a cell more than once?

You can start at any cell and move up, down, right, or left. When you have visited one type of insect, however, the next insect you visit must be of a different type.

ANSWER: PAGE **115**

Many respected mathematicians, such as Professor Ian Stewart, have tackled the shoelace problem below. The aim is to find the shortest path from the bottom left eyelet to the bottom right eyelet, passing through every eyelet only once. (Interestingly enough, the problem is really just a special case of the classic traveling salesman problem, which you may have encountered before.)

? DID YOU KNOW?

There are many ways to lace shoes. For a shoe with seven pairs of eyelets, there are about 400 million different ways to lace it!

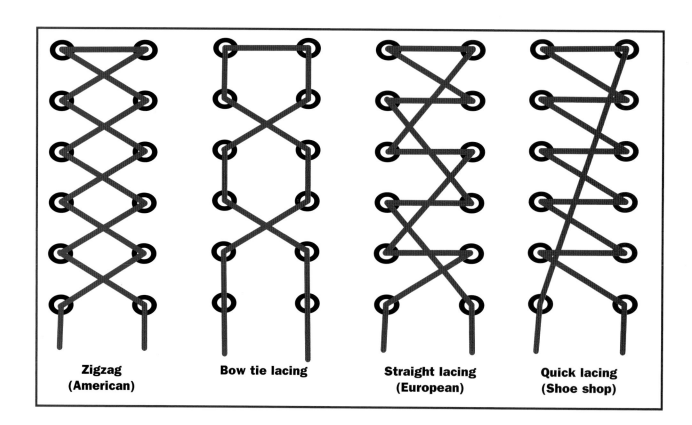

| Zigzag (American) | Bow tie lacing | Straight lacing (European) | Quick lacing (Shoe shop) |

▲ THE SHOELACE PROBLEM

What is the best way to lace your shoes? A few different ways are shown for a shoe with six pairs of eyelets.

Which is the shortest and which is the longest way to lace the shoe, if the laces must alternate between eyelets on the left and right side of the shoe?

ANSWER: PAGE **116**

◀ TOT UP A TON

Can you arrange the digits from 1 to 9 in succession, using each digit once only and inserting plus and minus signs as needed, to produce the sum of 100?

ANSWER: PAGE 116

▲ LET IT ROLL

What is the probability of rolling either a four or a six on a given toss of a die?

ANSWER: PAGE 116

The Hungarian mathematicians Esther Klein and Gyorgy Szekeres were the first to prove the theorem for the curious convex quadrilateral problem posed below. They got engaged and were married. Consequently, another Hungarian mathematician, Paul Erdös, named it the Happy End Problem. Endre Makai proved the theorem for a convex pentagon (see right).

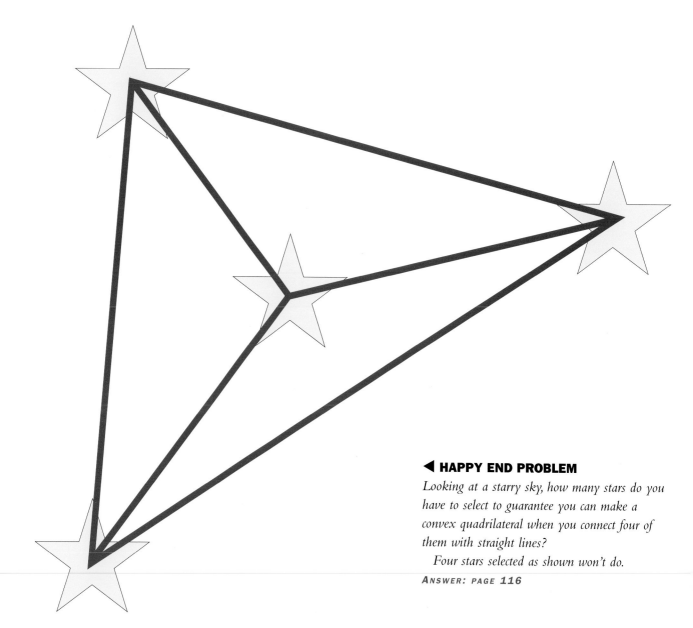

◀ HAPPY END PROBLEM

Looking at a starry sky, how many stars do you have to select to guarantee you can make a convex quadrilateral when you connect four of them with straight lines?

Four stars selected as shown won't do.

ANSWER: PAGE 116

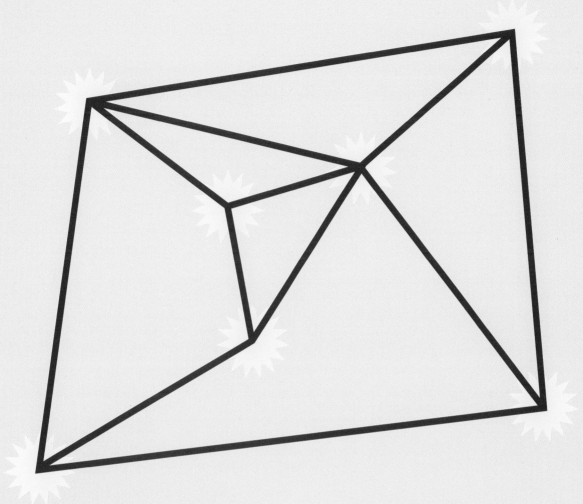

❄ Convex polygons

A polygon is convex if you can draw a straight line between *any* two points that remain inside the shape.

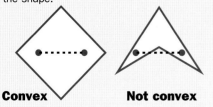

Convex   **Not convex**

▲ EVEN HAPPIER END

Once again looking at a starry sky, how many stars do you have to select to guarantee a convex pentagon when you connect them with straight lines?

Seven stars selected, as shown, won't solve the puzzle, no matter how the lines are connected.

ANSWER: PAGE 117

Graphs that possess no loops are called trees (because, like real trees, these graphs have branches that never link except through a trunk). Many processes that branch may be represented as trees. For example, the positions in a game of chess form a tree whose edges are the moves of the game. The strategy in many games is generally based on viewing the game as a tree, and computer programs that play such games as chess, checkers, and backgammon make essential use of this idea. Indeed, the advanced chess-playing computers that are capable of beating human grandmasters work out trees of possible moves; the computer then selects the move at the present point that will ensure the best possible outcome many moves into the future.

✳ Spanning trees

Put simply, a tree is a set of lines on which it is impossible to draw a closed loop. A tree that connects up all the available points (that is, doesn't leave any point isolated) is called a spanning tree.

Minimum spanning trees are of interest to mathematicians because they connect up every point as efficiently as possible, with each connection having a "weight" (analogous to cost).

An easy way to think about this is to consider a road network. The most useful yet lowest-cost road system possible would connect together every town using the cheapest set of road connections possible. In practice, however, this would lead to some very inconvenient routes for drivers. Hence, most road networks are not trees since loops are used.

▶ LOCAL AREA NETWORK

Problems often arise if we need to connect several points, but direct connection between each pair of points is not necessary.

One way of networking these eight computers is shown on the right, with the edges indicating the length of the wiring between each.

Can you connect the eight computers in a more efficient way?

ANSWER: PAGE 117

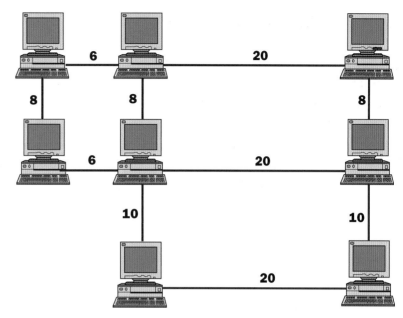

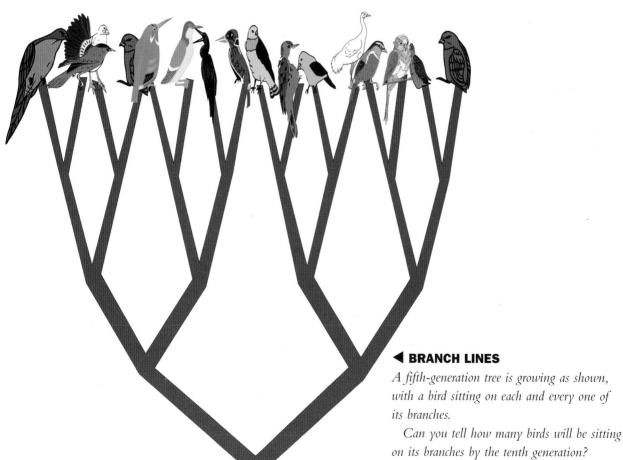

◀ BRANCH LINES

A fifth-generation tree is growing as shown, with a bird sitting on each and every one of its branches.

Can you tell how many birds will be sitting on its branches by the tenth generation?

ANSWER: PAGE 117

Vertex coloring of a graph involves coloring each vertex (point of intersection) so that no two edges will connect two identically colored vertices. The aim is to find out the minimal number of colors needed to achieve this objective.

▼ TRIAL SEPARATION

What is the minimum number of colors needed to vertex color the graph below?

ANSWER: PAGE **118**

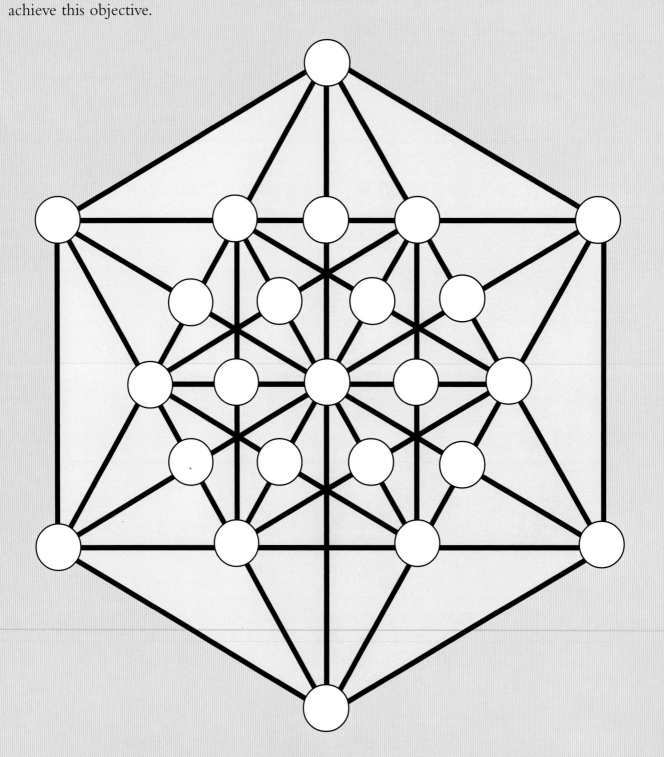

▼ FISH OUT OF WATER

Six tropical fish have to be placed in a certain number of aquariums because some are not compatible with each other.

The uncolored graph represents the compatibility situation, with its vertices representing the six fish. Each of the edges connects fish who fight with each other.

How many aquariums are needed to place the six fish safely in water?

How can vertex coloring of the graph help?

ANSWER: PAGE 118

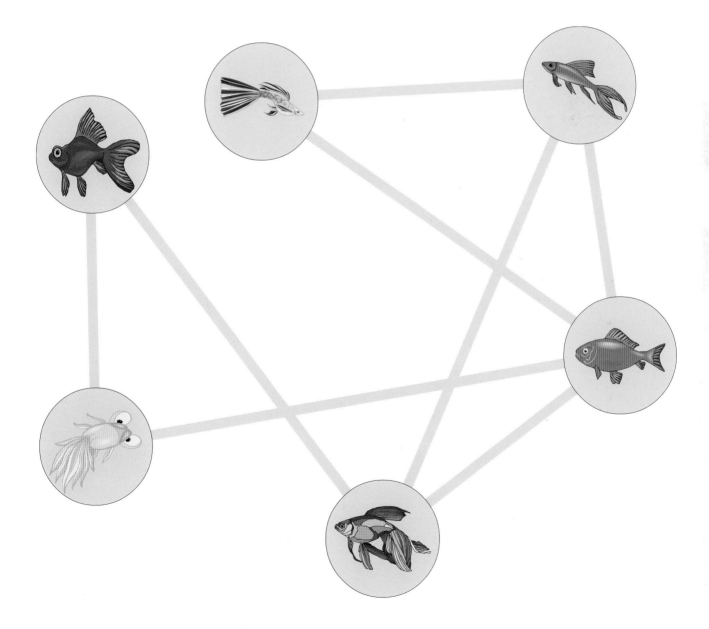

Here's another collection of small, varied problems to tease you. This time we're testing your ability with three kinds of number crunching: averages, percentages, and iteration (the study of repetition).

▶ COMMUTER COMPUTATION

Yesterday, I traveled to work at my usual average of about 56 mph (90 km/h). However, coming home there was constuction holding up the traffic, so on my return journey I averaged only 28 mph (45 km/h).

What was my average speed for the round trip?

ANSWER: PAGE 119

◀ A SUITE DEAL?

The saleslady sold two sofas at the bargain price of $1,200 apiece.

She made a 25% profit on the first sofa and a 20% loss on the other. She assumed that she still made a profit on the combined sale. Was she right in this assumption?

ANSWER: PAGE 119

▶ THE GRADUATE

The top graduate of his class had a choice of two offers—both at $10,000 a year.

Unable to make up his mind between the two offers, he wrote to the two companies asking what his chances were for raises over the next five years.

Company 1's answer was a guaranteed raise of $300 every six months for the first five years.

Company 2's answer, on the other hand, was a guaranteed raise of $1,200 every twelve months for the first five years.

To the astonishment of his parents, the graduate accepted company 1's offer. Was his choice the right one?

ANSWER: PAGE 119

There are many unique ways you can fill in this diagram using two blocks of color. By taking these pieces and using them with their reflections, you can play a neat dominoes game.

▼ SAMPLE GAME

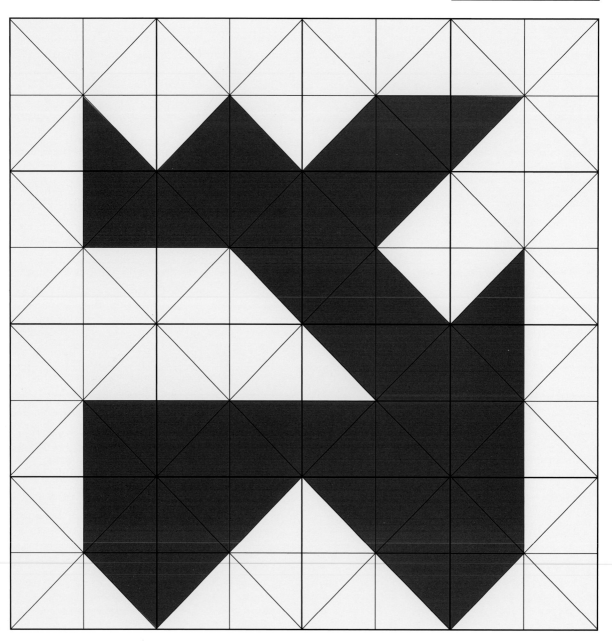

▶ THE RED CENTER

Can you arrange the 16 colored squares at right in a 4-by-4 square pattern so that all the red areas will merge into one big red area, all of which will be inside the outlines of the 4-by-4 square, with the exception of red points, which are allowed to touch the outline?

One of the many solutions is shown on page 64.

Have fun trying to find the others!

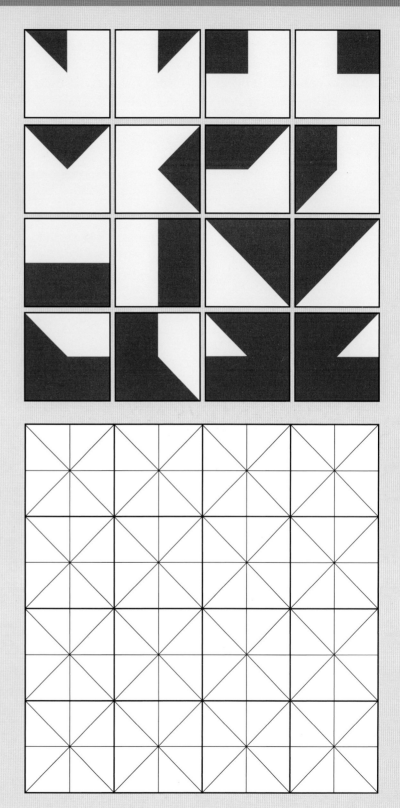

If you examine both of the figures on these pages carefully, you should find ways of dividing up the area into more manageable "chunks" that the eye can comprehend. We hope this advice will lead you to the correct solution in both cases.

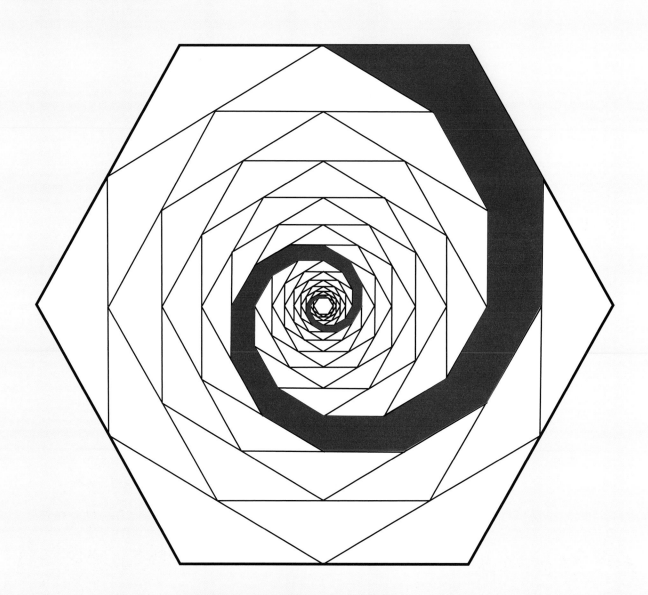

▲ YOU ARE FEELING VERY SLEEPY...

What is the area of the red spiral arm as a proportion of the entire hexagon?

ANSWER: PAGE 119

▶ SQUARE DIVISION

Three identical squares inscribed in an equilateral triangle dissect it into 22 regions as shown.

Using three other identical squares, can you do better?

ANSWER: PAGE 119

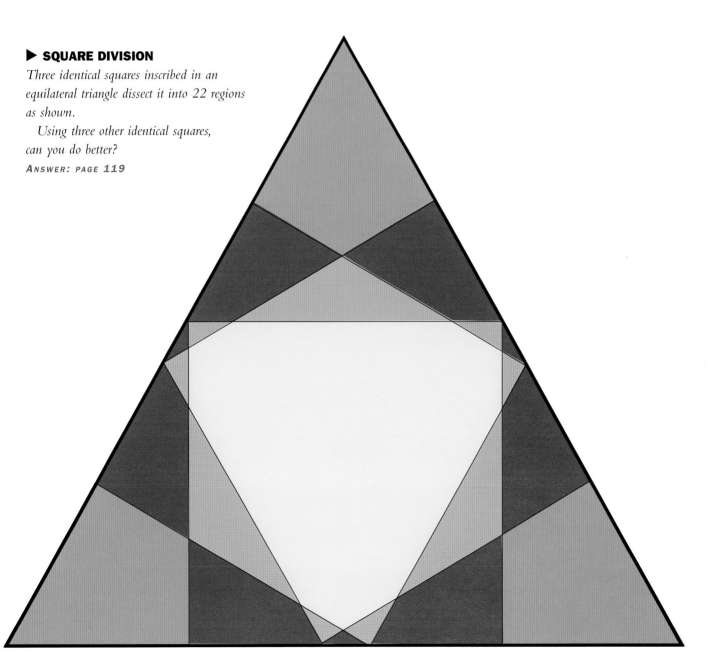

The science of making accurate, two-dimensional drawings of three-dimensional forms and of graphically solving problems relating to the size and position in space of such forms is called descriptive geometry. It forms the basis of much of engineering and architectural drafting.

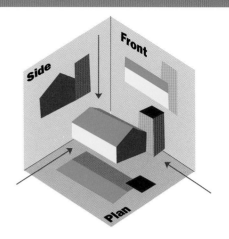

✳ Descriptive geometry

Everyone should have a basic understanding of descriptive drawings.

One of the most useful usual techniques of representing lines, surfaces, or solids in plane drawings is by means of orthographic drawing or orthographic projection. The literal meaning of "orthographic" is "perpendicular."

Orthographic drawings are based on three or more views of an object as shown in the figures. In this type of projection, the object to be represented is referred to one or more imaginary planes that are at right angles to one another. A point in space is represented by the point in the reference plane touched by a ray perpendicular to the plane and passing through that point.

Orthographic drawings are like an international language, extensively used in engineering, design, and architecture, because they can clearly and accurately describe complex forms.

Technicians and engineers anywhere can "read" orthographic drawings, because they have become standardized forms of pictorial visual communications.

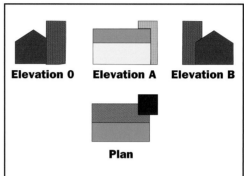

Elevation 0   **Elevation A**   **Elevation B**

Plan

First angle projection (standard throughout Europe except the Netherlands)

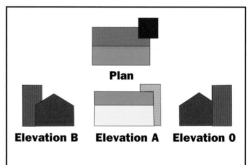

Plan

Elevation B   **Elevation A**   **Elevation 0**

British standard projection

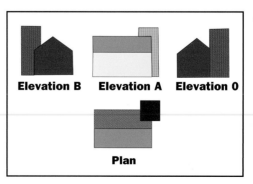

Elevation B   **Elevation A**   **Elevation 0**

Plan

Third-angle projection (used in the Netherlands and U.S.A.)

Isometric drawing

Another standard form of visual pictorial communication is the isometric drawing. Isometric drawings portray three-dimensional forms on a two-dimensional page.

Orthographic drawing or projections can be developed from an isometric drawing or vice versa.

The word "isometric" means equal measure, and refers to the equal angles used in the drawings.

An isometric cube is shown here, demonstrating the standard angles in isometric drawings. In the real cube the edges would be at 90° to one another. Using the conventional 60° and 120° angles allows us to potray the cube in a way that resembles a perspective view with a minimum of distortion and without the complexities of the converging lines found in perspective drawing.

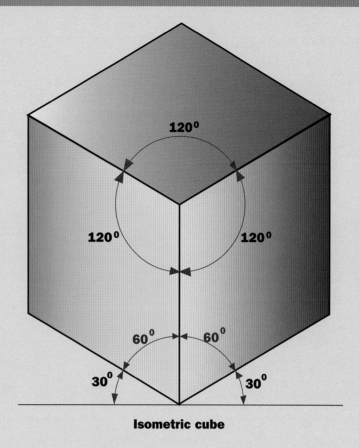

Isometric cube

The isometric drawing on the bottom left shows the same object as the three separate views of the orthographic drawing, below right.

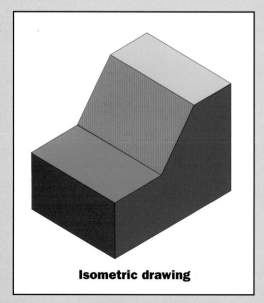

Isometric drawing

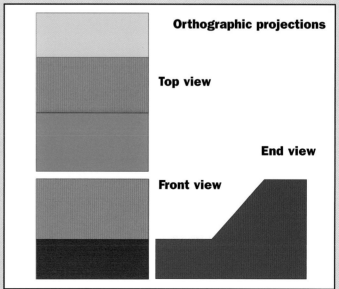

Orthographic projections

Top view

End view

Front view

▼ HERE'S THE PLAN 1

In each case, select the set of orthographic projections
corresponding to the isometric drawing of the object.

ANSWER: PAGE 120

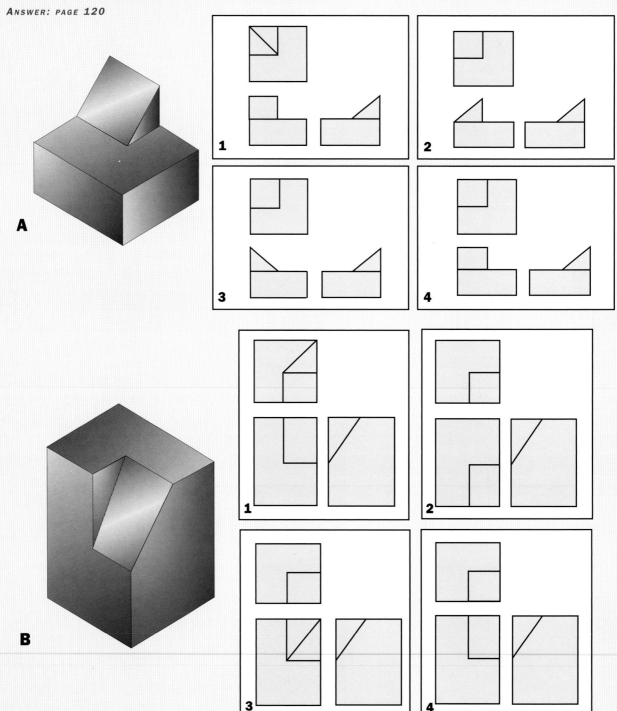

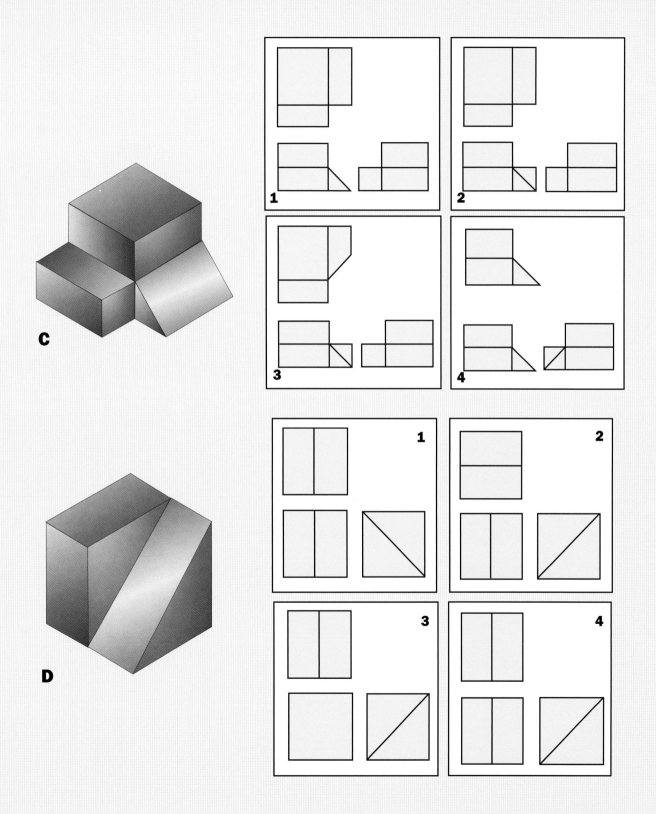

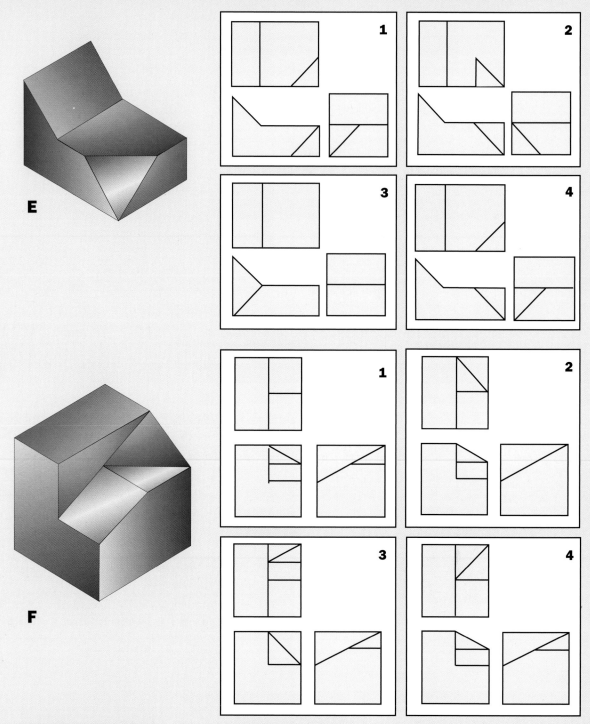

E

F

▲ **HERE'S THE PLAN 2**

As on pages 70–71, select the set of orthographic projections corresponding to the isometric drawing of the object.

ANSWER: PAGE 120

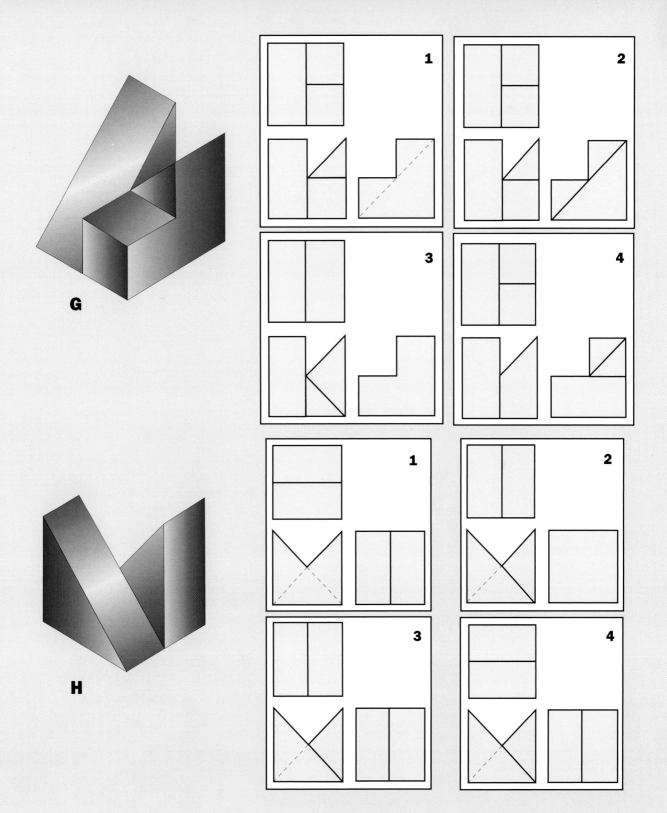

▼ CAN I HAVE YOUR ORTHOGRAPHIC?

The object here is to draw in the orthographic projections of the isometric drawing of the three-dimensional solid. (Hint: 6 has a square base.) Try to complete all the puzzles on pages 74–77 before looking at the answers.

ANSWER: PAGE 120

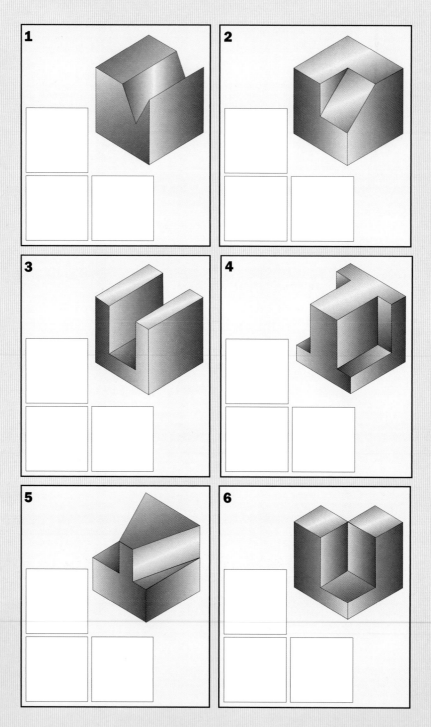

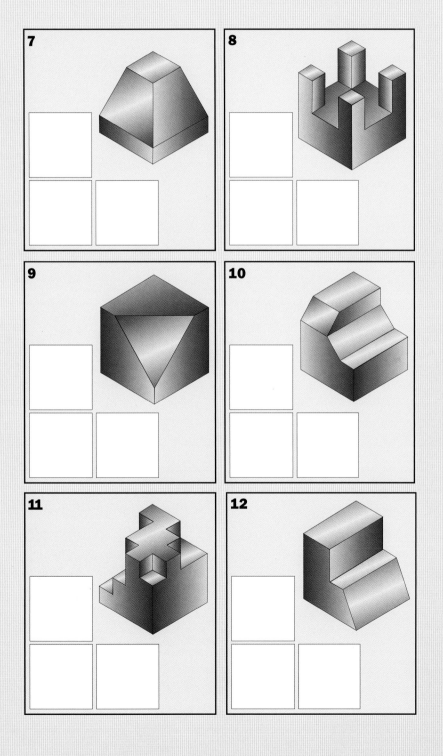

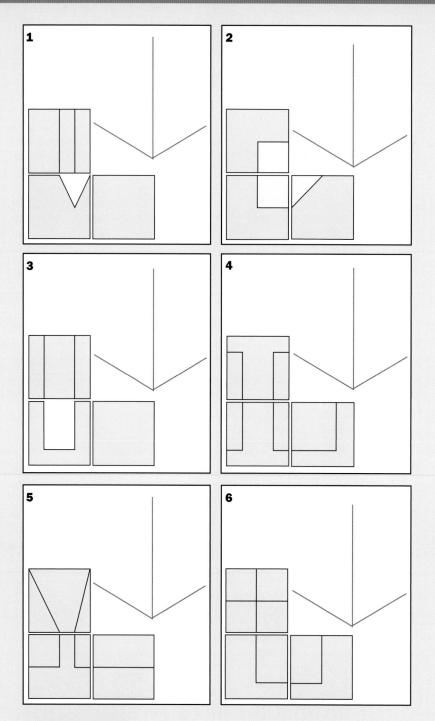

▲ SOLID STATE

In each case, can you imagine how the isometric drawings of the solids shown by their orthographic projections should look?

ANSWER: PAGE *120*

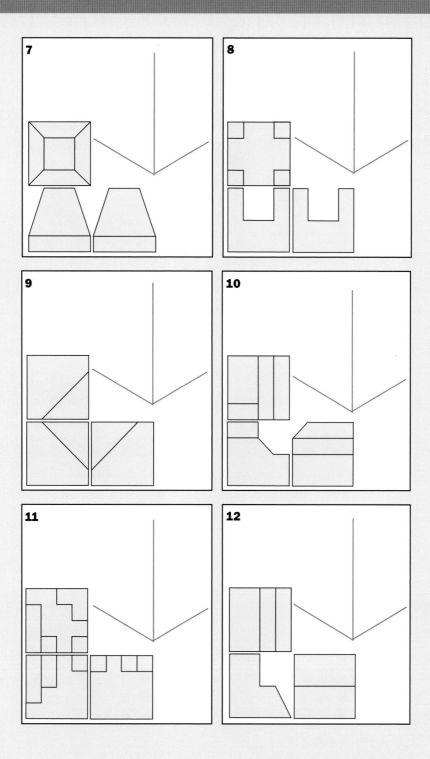

A kite is a "planar convex quadrilateral consisting of two adjacent sides of length a and the other two sides of length b." Alternatively, it's a diamond of fabric with some string on the end. I know which one I'd rather play with.

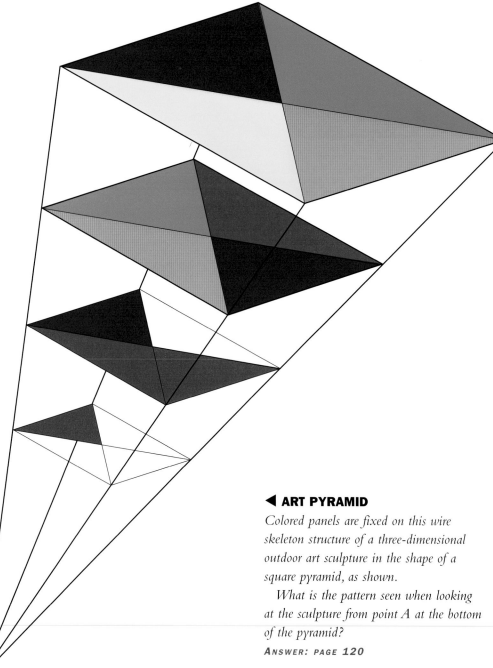

◄ ART PYRAMID

Colored panels are fixed on this wire skeleton structure of a three-dimensional outdoor art sculpture in the shape of a square pyramid, as shown.

What is the pattern seen when looking at the sculpture from point A at the bottom of the pyramid?

ANSWER: PAGE 120

▶ THE VIEW FROM ABOVE

The top view of a building is shown here from above.

Can you envisage and sketch the three-dimensional form of the top of the building as seen from above?

ANSWER: PAGE 120

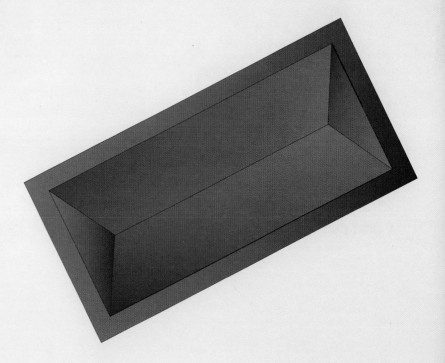

Here's another chance to have a go at our Find the Shapes game. This time the pattern is more intricate. But will that make the shapes harder or easier to find? Only one way to find out…

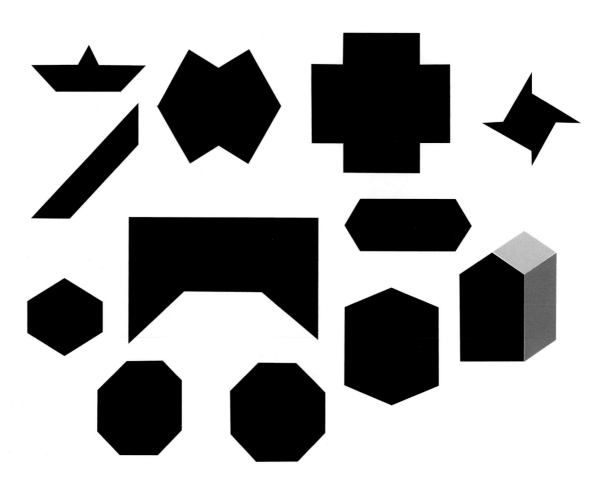

▲ HIDE AND SEEK

How long will it take you to find the hidden figures above in the colored pattern on the right?

   The shapes may overlap several colored regions, but they can all be found in the same size and orientation in the pattern.

   It is sometimes surprisingly difficult to find familiar shapes and figures when they are hidden in unfamiliar surroundings.

ANSWER: PAGE **121**

The breeding patterns of rabbits, growth of shellfish, and flight pattern of crows can all be described in mathematical terms. So, perhaps it's no surprise that here we're dealing with horses, dogs, turtles, and, um, extra-terrestrials.

$$\sqrt{49} \times \sqrt{36}$$

Clever hans and roger the dog

Clever Hans was a horse owned by a German teacher named Osten. In 1904 Clever Hans was known throughout the world since he was, as the newspapers of the time referred to him, "a horse with unusual mathematical thinking abilities."

Oskar Pfungst, the researcher, described Hans thus: "A horse that could solve arithmetical problems, and also could read and understand spoken German."

After many months, he discovered the true source of Hans's cleverness, however: the horse watched for slight involuntary cues that invariably arose from his audience as he approached the correct number of taps of his hoof.

Until that discovery, Hans gave a devastating blow to the idea that human beings were uniquely intelligent.

Soon afterward, however, there appeared a dog named Roger, who could seemingly play cards (and win), as well as solve arithmetical problems!

◀ TIM'S TURTLE

Tim found 14 bricks from which to construct a wall in the garden for his new pet, a small turtle.

As his turtle grew, Tim wanted to enlarge the enclosure as much as possible, using the same number of bricks. How could he do this?

ANSWER: PAGE 122

▶ ALIEN-NATION

The population of the world in 2999 is dominated by aliens and consists of either aliens or human beings dressed in alien disguise.

The aliens are incapable of telling a lie, and the human beings are all equally incapable of telling the truth.

The one on the left (1), identifies himself to the one in the middle (2), who tells the one on the right (3): "He says he is an alien."

"No, he is not an alien—he is a human being," answers the one on the right (3).

Can you tell whether there are more aliens or human beings in the group?

ANSWER: PAGE 122

Mathematics is a universal language and its symbols also have a wider application outside the discipline of mathematics. You may be surprised by how many of these you know.

▼ STATUS SYMBOLS: A QUIZ

Can you work out which term matches which symbol on the cards marked 1–50?

ANSWER: PAGE *123*

THE TERMS

Acute angle	*Cone*	*Equal to*	*Infinity*	*Parallelepiped*
And so on	*Congruent to*	*Equal to or*	*Intersecting circles*	*Parallelogram*
Approaches (in value)	*Corresponds to*	* greater than*	*Isosceles triangle*	*Plus or minus*
Approximately	*Cube*	*Equal to or less than*	*Less than*	*Pyramid*
* equal to*	*Cuboid*	*Equilateral triangle*	*Not equal to*	*Radius*
Circle	*Cylinder*	*Kite*	*Obtuse angle*	*Regular heptagon*
Circumference	*Diameter*	*Identically equal to*	*Octahedron*	*Regular hexagon*
				Regular nonagon
				Regular octagon
				Regular pentagon
				Rhombus
				Right angle
				Right triangle
				Scalene triangle
				Sector
				Segment
				Similar to
				* (proportional)*
				Sphere
				Square root
				Sum of terms
				Tangent
				Tetrahedron
				Therefore
				Trapezoid

1 ∞

2 →

3 • • •

4 ≤

5 =

6 ∴

7 Σ

8 ≥

9 <

10 √

11 ~

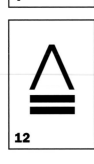

12 ≜

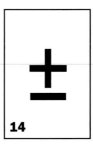

13 ⊗

14 ±

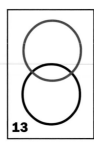

15 ≈

◀ ▶ **THE SYMBOLS**

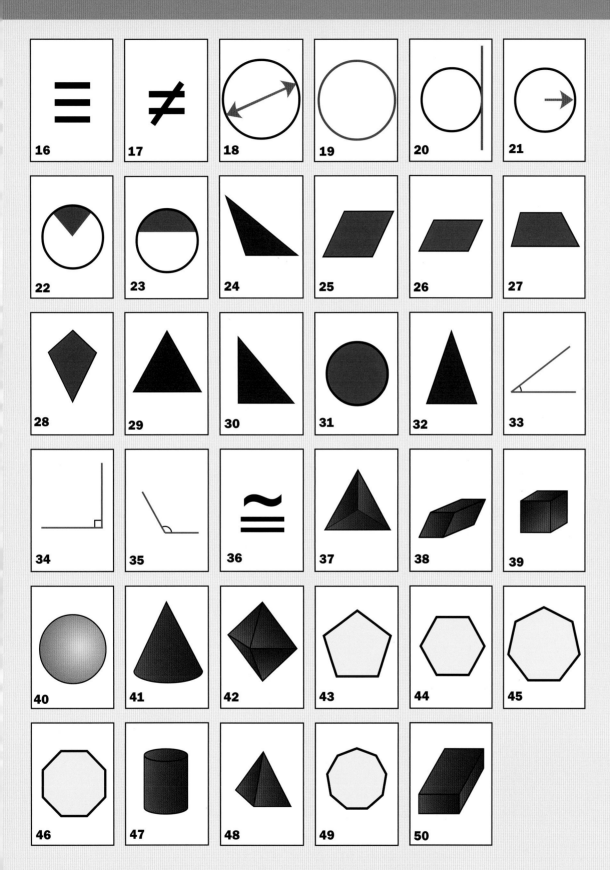

Only your imagination is the limit to creating an endless number of pleasing symmetrical and nonsymmetrical abstract patterns with this colorful clown game.

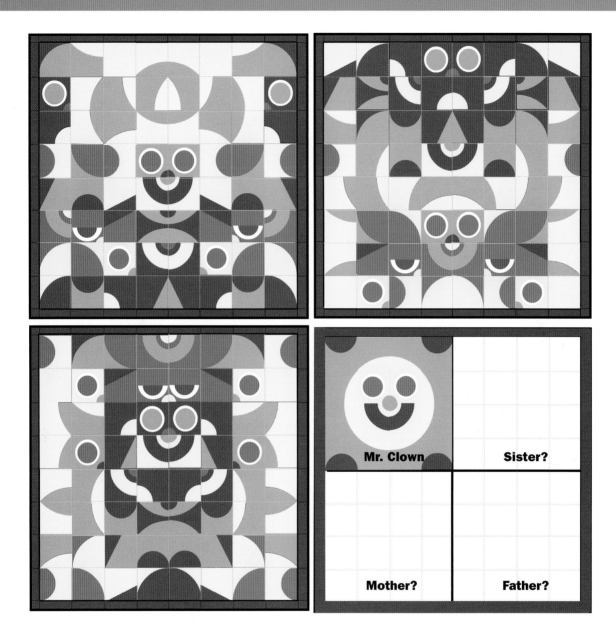

▲ CLOWN AND COMPANY

The Puzzle Mr. Clown and his family are hiding in the abstract pattern at left, formed by 64 square tiles. Copy, cut out, and rearrange the 64 square tiles to reveal the four members of the family: Mr. Clown and his father, mother, and sister (will they look like my results?).

Each is symmetrical and made up of 16 tiles.

Can you believe that the "surrealistic" images above are all the results of random scrambling of the four members of the clown family?

The Game You can also play a number of games. Divide the 64 tiles into two identical groups. Players alternate turns by placing a tile in an 8-by-8 gameboard, observing vertical bilateral symmetry rules, until all the tiles have been placed. The resulting picture is somehow always an esthetic surprise.

Or how about devising a memory game? Or other games of your own inventions and rules?

ANSWER: PAGE 123

The earliest traces of origami (paper-folding) come from Japan. During A.D. 794–1185, known as the Heian Period, abstract folded symbols were used in the Shinto religion.

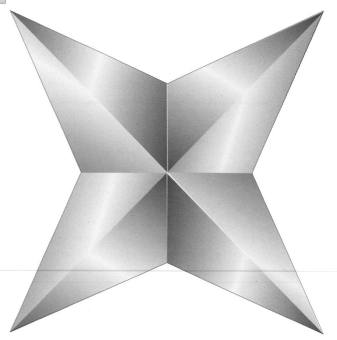

▶ **FOUR-POINTED STAR**

The object here is to fold a square piece of paper and with one single straight cut create a perfect four-pointed star, as shown, when unfolding the paper.

How many folds will be required?

ANSWER: PAGE **124**

▼ SIX-POINTED STAR

The object this time is to fold a square piece of paper and with one single straight cut create a perfect six-pointed star, as shown, when unfolding the paper.

How many folds will be required?

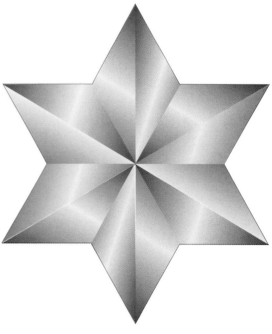

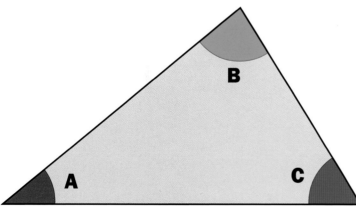

◄ LUTHER'S PROOF

Euclid proved that the three angles of a triangle always add up to a straight angle (that is, 180 degrees).

The beauty of mathematics is that often amateurs, with a bit of insight, can make new discoveries and proofs.

Luther Washington, for example, today a mathematician at Stanford, as a very young student had an idea to prove it in a simpler way, using a pencil only.

Can you work out how he did it?

ANSWER: PAGE **125**

When a particular shape is able to cover an infinite flat surface without leaving any gaps, we say that it "tessellates." There are only three regular polygons with the ability to tessellate—the triangle, the square, and the hexagon.

▼ CROSS THE CAUSEWAY

In this game for two players, the Red player fills in any blank shape with a red marker, then the Green player shades in another shape with a green pen. Players take turns until the Red player wins by connecting the Red banks via a solid red path, or likewise for the Green player. The black areas are out of bounds.

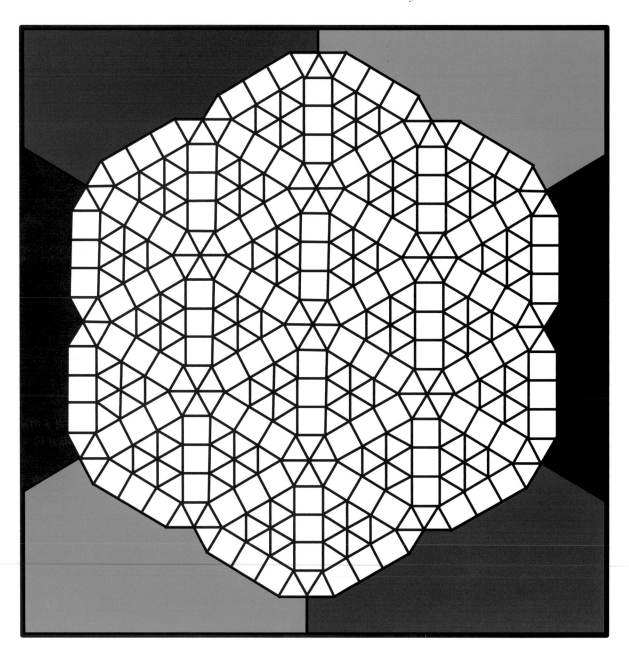

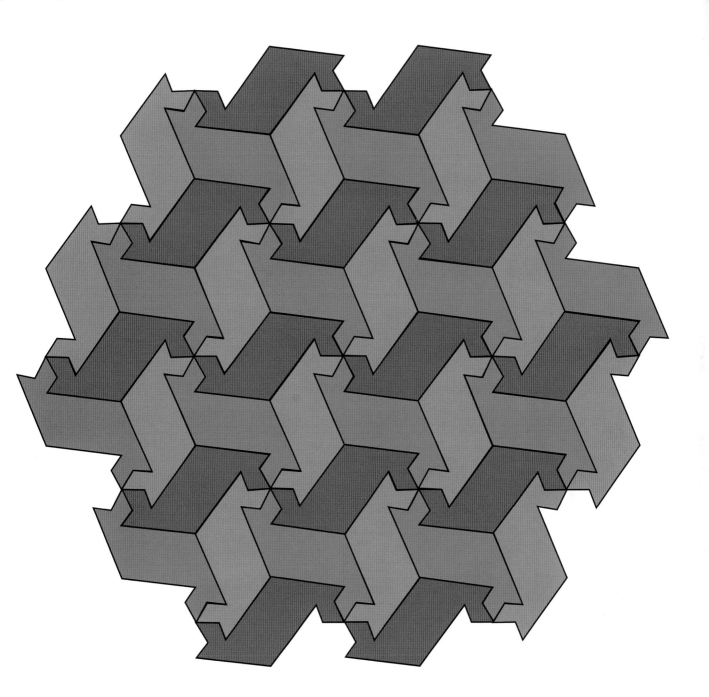

▲ SIX-SIDED SYMMETRY

Complex tessellating (tiling) patterns can be obtained from simple elements. What is not so obvious is that this pattern was created using one single hexagonal patterned tile.

Can you discover the outlines of the hexagonal tiles?

ANSWER: PAGE 125

Grab your pencils and get ready for some wordplay and a chance to indulge in a spot of triangulation.

▼ ANAGRAM GRID

The anagram grid is a novel paper-and-pencil wordgame, ideal as a solitaire, as well as a competiton game for a number of players. Its basic concept can be easily understood from the sample shown on the right. In the first row the eight letters of the solution appear in a random order. The goal of the puzzle is to use the same eight letters to form different words in each row according to the number of blank cells available.

You are not allowed to repeat words. Points are scored for each word you can find, plus an extra eight points for the right solution at the end. What will you score on the 10-letter anagram grid?

ANSWER: PAGE **126**

An 8-letter sample anagram grid.

A sample solution scoring 21 points.

The 10-letter anagram grid.

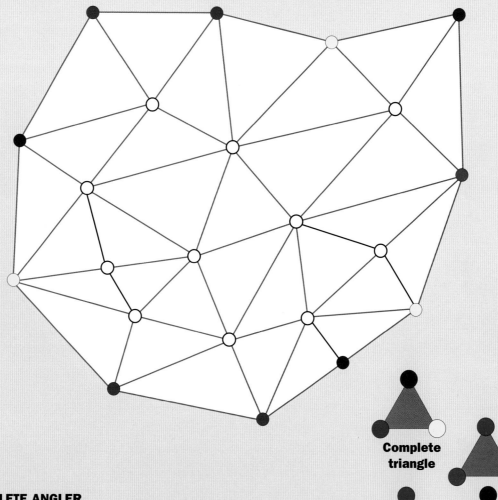

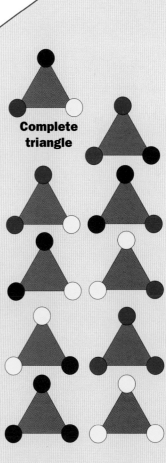

Complete triangle

▲ THE COMPLETE ANGLER

Draw a polygon of any number of sides. Place a dot at each of the corners, and then place any number of dots at random on the border or the inside.

Then, using the dots as corners, divide the polygon into nonoverlapping triangles and label their corners in any way, using three colors—red, blue, and yellow.

Coloring the triangles in this way means there can be ten different types of triangles as shown at right. A triangle with three colors at its vertices is a complete triangle

In my example I have colored only the border dots.

Can you color all the remaining dots so that there are exactly two complete triangles?

ANSWER: PAGE 126

Lines might look boring, but their significance in mapmaking, physics, art, sports, and even palmistry is important. So here are a couple of puzzles that celebrate the humble line.

> Science answers the question WHY, and Art the question WHY NOT.
>
> **Sol LeWitt, artist**

▲ FLY THE FLAG

Cut out the 16 square tiles and rearrange them in another 4-by-4 configuration so that every line follows on without interruption from one side of the big square to the other, including the two main diagonals.

ANSWER: PAGE **127**

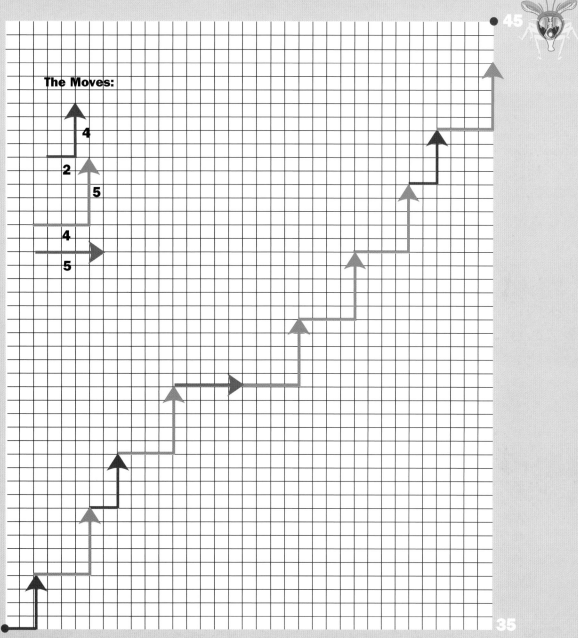

The Moves:

4
2
5
4
5

45

35

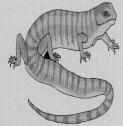

▲ FLAG THE FLY

The lizard starts at the bottom of the grid and moves along the intersections in an attempt to catch the fly shown at the top. His moves can be of any of the three types shown in the inset.

How might he do it? (A path is demonstrated above that falls short of the fly by only three square units.)

Answer: page 127

And so we've reached the end. Find your own way out, will you? Just follow the arrows—it's as simple as that.

▲ AN ARROW ESCAPE

Using the 24 arrow blocks positioned as they are here, start anywhere and visit cells by following the directions pointed out by the arrows from cell to cell horizontally, vertically, or diagonally.

How many cells can you visit in a continuous path without visiting any cell more than once?

ANSWER: PAGE 127

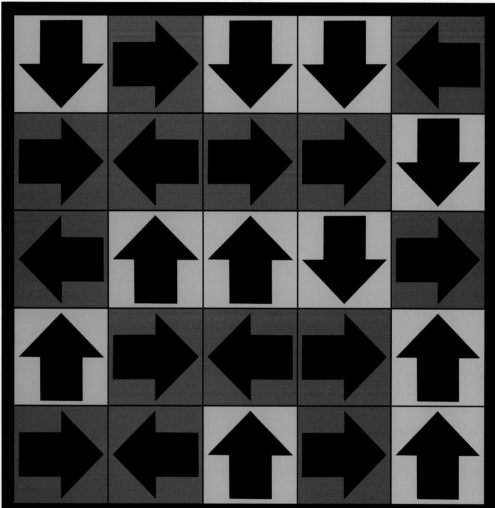

▲ AT NO POINT...

Can you find a path visiting each cell of this 5-by-5 grid matrix, moving horizontally and vertically in a continuous line without crossing any cell more than once and without encountering any arrow head-on?

In other words, you can move in any direction, but the arrow on the square on which you you land must not point to the square from which you have just come.

ANSWER: PAGE 128

POETRY CIRCLE (page 6)

"A BIT OF VIRTUE WILL NEVER HURT YOU"

The sentence is formed by taking the letters in order of the increasing size of the letter squares.

HISTORY MYSTERY (page 7)

Problem 79 in the Rhind Papyrus relates to a geometric progression, and it is perhaps the world's oldest puzzle. The solution is the geometric progression of five terms, of which the first term is 7, and the multiplier is also 7:

houses	7
cats	49
mice	343
ears	2,401
flour	16,807 (the answer)

NO EYE DEAR (page 9)

The answer lies in taking the use of plurals literally.

The man had only one eye (so he didn't have "eyes").

The tree had only two apples on it.

He took only one, and left only one on the tree (so he didn't leave "apples").

ST. IVES RIDDLE (page 9)

Only one.

All the others were coming *from* St. Ives.

WINDOW BOX (page 11)

The top-left corner of the pattern is at point 21 across, 15 down.

MYSTERY SIGNS 1 (page 12)

The letters are rotated in place, spelling the sentence "Play is fun."

MYSTERY SIGNS 2 (page 13)

The missing sign is number 8 (∞).

The number sequence from 1 to 9 appears rotated and in mirror-image.

PAPER VIEW 1 (page 14)

1. A
2. D
3. D

PAPER VIEW 2 (page 15)

1. C
2. B
3. C

▼ SWEET SIXTEEN (page 16)

Among the 14 different possible solutions (not counting rotations or reflections as different), there are two symmetrical patterns, and four solutions with the smallest number of intersections (two).

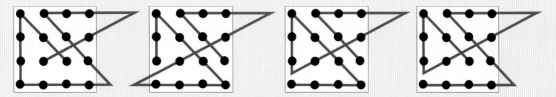

Puzzle 2: the four solutions with the smallest number of intersections (2).

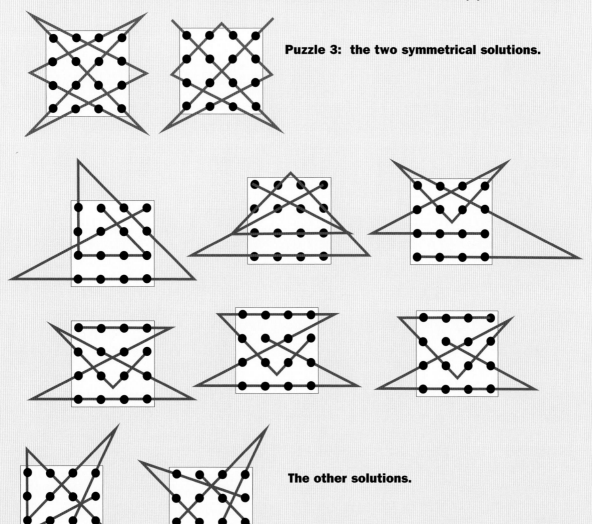

Puzzle 3: the two symmetrical solutions.

The other solutions.

▶ TWENTY-FIVE SENSE
(page 17)

Here we show a solution with 34 connecting lines. Can you do better? If not, do you know why not?

Six potential lines were left unconnected.

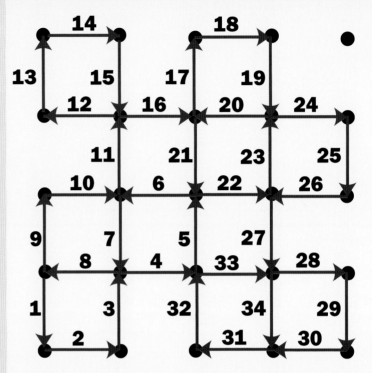

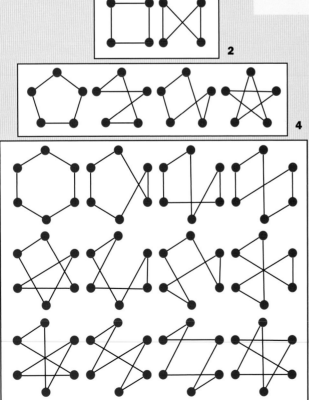

◀ ALL THE RIGHT CONNECTIONS
(page 17)

There are two solutions for four points; four solutions for five points; and twelve solutions for six points, as shown.

▼ PLANT PLOT (FOR K = 3)
(page 18)

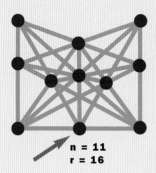

n = 11
r = 16

▼ PLANT PLOT (FOR K = 4)
(page 18)

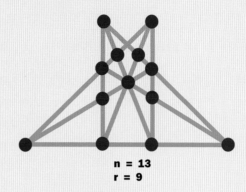

n = 13
r = 9

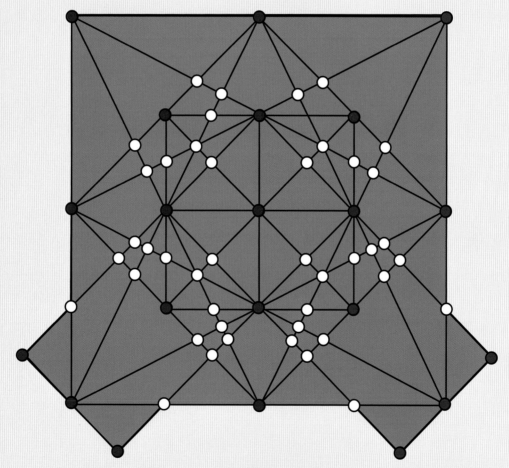

▲ TREE-MENDOUS (page 19)

You will need 21 red counters, forming 30 rows of 3 counters on each straight line.

▼ PICTURE STRIP (page 20)

Rotate every strip by 180 degrees. The shaded squares will now be in the positions marked here in black. They form a simple picture of someone playing soccer.

Stage 1

Push each row to the right until the first square in the row matches a top or bottom edge of one of the squares in the row on either side of it. Where a match isn't possible (for example, with the duck's tail) don't move that row.

◀ LOOK OUT! (page 21)

The end result is shown. The trick is to move the rows and columns of squares until the first square (from the side you are pushing) matches at least one side of the inner fixed squares.

If a match isn't possible in a given row or column, don't move it.

Stage 3

Now move each row to the left until the square you're pushing (on your right-hand side) gets a color match.

Stage 2

Now repeat the same thing, moving each column upward until you get a color match.

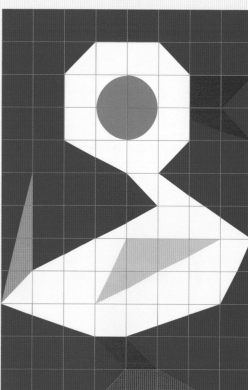

Stage 4

Finally, push each column down until the top square matches the side of another square on either side of it.

▼ FLASHPOINT (page 22)

One solution is shown. For the other solution: In move 2, hiker 2 crosses back.

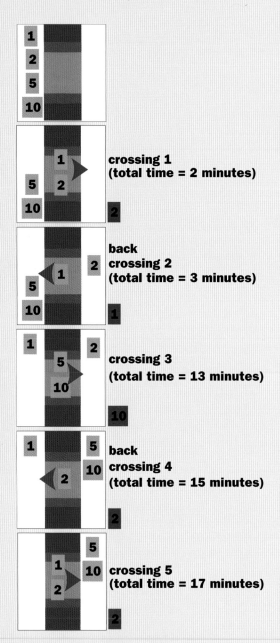

crossing 1
(total time = 2 minutes)

back
crossing 2
(total time = 3 minutes)

crossing 3
(total time = 13 minutes)

back
crossing 4
(total time = 15 minutes)

crossing 5
(total time = 17 minutes)

SWEEEET (page 23)

Cake = $1.75; Sundae = $0.75

SNAIL'S PACE (page 23)

The snail ends up 4 units higher after each day and night. After 20 full days, it will be 20 × 4 units = 80 units up the window. There are only 10 units left to travel. So, on day 21 it will easily reach the top and that's it—there's no need to consider the slide back. So 21 days is the answer.

▼ SIX SPOT (page 24)

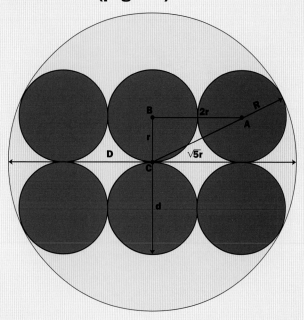

To answer the puzzle, look at the artwork above. Because A is the center of a circle and all six smaller circles are in a regular pattern, it's easy to deduce that the line AB is at right angles to the line BC. In other words, ABC is a right-angled triangle. If r is the radius of a small circle, then AB is 2r, and BC is r long. Using the Pythagorean theorem:

AC is $\sqrt{(AB^2 + BC^2)} + \sqrt{(2r^2 + r^2)} = \sqrt{5}\,r$

Then, if we look at point A to the edge of the large circle, we can see that it this is the radius of a small circle, which is r long. Adding these two together, we obtain $(\sqrt{5} + 1) \times r$. If we divide this by the diameter of a small circle (2r), we get $(\sqrt{5} + 1)/2$, which is approximately 1.618. This is called the golden ratio and it pops up in all manner of unexpected places in number theory and geometry.

▶ TRICKY TRIANGLE (page 25)

Each triangular number is bigger than the previous one by the number of circles on its bottom row, which is the next natural number.

We can tilt the triangular pattern and add to it its mirror-image to form a rectangular pattern as shown on the right.

The 17th triangular number can easily be obtained by:

$$n \times (n + 1)/2$$
$$[17 \times (17 + 1)]/2 = 153$$

This is an ingenious shortcut to obtain the sum of any number of natural numbers. The 40th triangular number is $(40 \times 41)/2 = 820$.

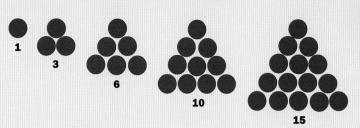

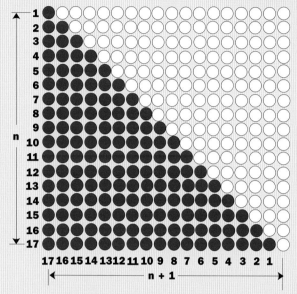

BACK IN THE FOLD (page 27)

A. 4
B. 1
C. 2
D. 3
E. 2

SEATING ARRANGEMENT (page 28)

There are eight different ways to seat men and women in a row, avoiding women sitting next to each other.

W M M W
W M W M
M W M W
W M M M
M W M M
M M W M
M M M W
M M M M

When the number of chairs, "n," is 1, 2, 3, 4, 5... the answers are 2, 3, 5, 8, 13..., and so on.

(Interestingly enough, this is in accord with the Fibonacci number sequence, where each term is the sum of the previous two numbers.)

▼ BLANKET COVERAGE (page 29)

It's actually a regular octagon that has been repeated many times.

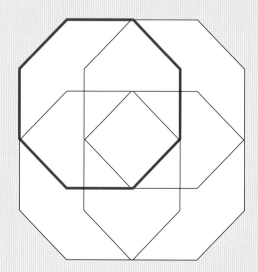

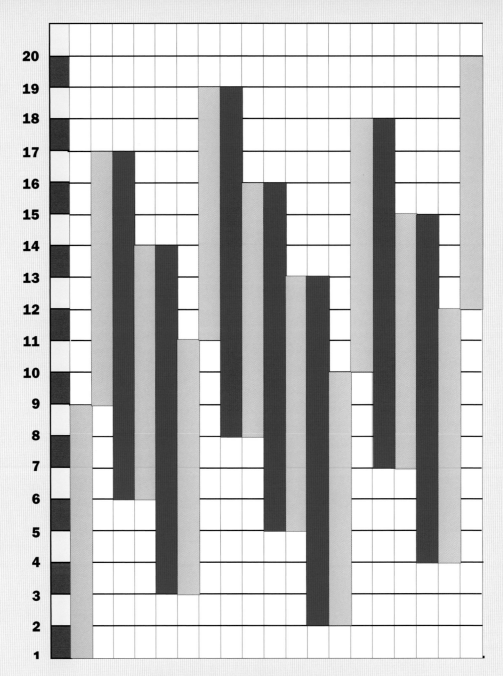

▲ AN UP AND DOWN CAREER (PAGE 30)

It is possible to visit all floors of the building (up journeys are shown in light blue, down journeys in dark blue).

The minimum number of journeys to visit all floors is of course 19 and the floors will be visited in the following sequence:
1–9–17–6–14–3–11–19–8–16–5–13–2–10–18–7–15–4–12–20.

RIGHT THIS WAY (page 31)

The sequence goes wrong at the third tile in the fourth row.

▶ INSIDE MOLE (page 32)

The rule was: Go forward 1 block then turn right, then go forward 2 blocks then turn right, forward 3 blocks and turn right, etc. until the mole counts up to 9 blocks. The mole then starts again for a second series of 1 to 9 block movements. However, when he starts the third series from "1" again, he chooses to turn left instead of right. That's the point where he breaks the rule (marked with a blue cross).

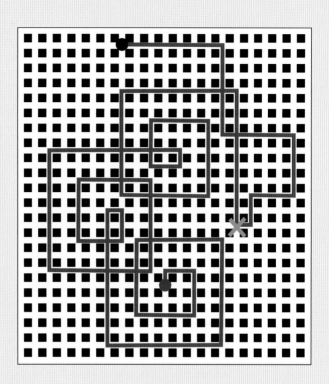

▼ PATHFINDER (page 33)

There are 14 paths as shown.

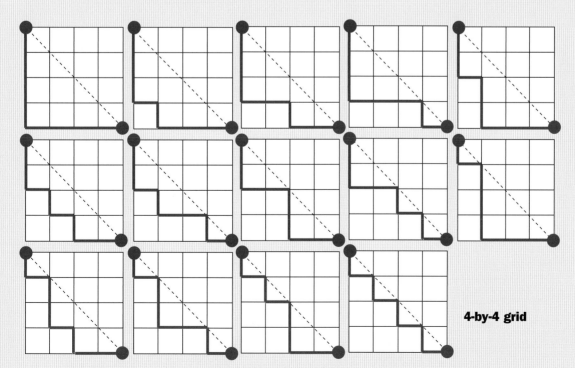

4-by-4 grid

5 **13** **12**

◀ GOLDEN JUBILEE (page 34)

Taking into account the Pythagorean relationship, the amount of gold in the two smaller plaques is the same as in the big one. So there is no difference.

It is a lesser-known fact that the Pythagorean theorem holds for any set of geometrically similar figures drawn on the three sides of a right-angled triangle.

The validity of this so-called generalized form of the Pythagorean theorem relates not only to areas but also to the volumes of the figures if their thicknesses are identical.

WHO IS A MILLIONAIRE? (page 35)

1. The person who is 1,000,000 hours old is 114 years old.
2. The person who is 1,000,000 minutes old is about 2 years old.
3. The person who is 1,000,000 seconds old is a baby just over $11\frac{1}{2}$ days old.
4. The woman must be the odd one out, as she is clearly none of these.

FIRE DRILL (page 35)

If the middle rung is labeled "zero," then the fireman went up three rungs to number 3, down five rungs to number −2, then up seven rungs to number 5. Finally he went up six more rungs to the top.

So the top must have been 11 rungs above the middle. Add to this the 11 rungs below the middle, and the middle rung itself, and the answer is 23 rungs.

ID PARADE (page 36)

Since Mac was in the middle of the lineup, an odd number of inmates took part. Since Jim was 20th, there must have been at least 21 inmates. Mac's position must have been an odd number lower than 13, so he was 11th and there were 21 inmates in line.

TRICKY TELEPATHY (page 37)

No matter which two-digit number you chose, the outcome will always be one of the following numbers: 9, 18, 27, 36, 45, 54, 63, 72, or 81.

All these numbers are accompanied by a blue color, as predicted.

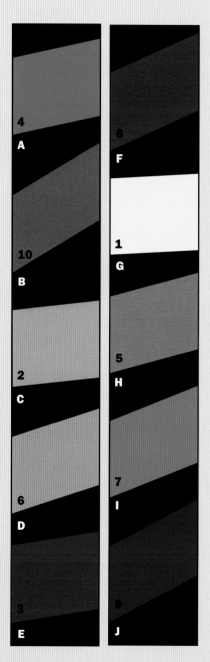

◄ STOPGAPS (page 38)

A	4
B	10
C	2
D	6
E	3
F	8
G	1
H	5
I	7
J	9

▶ FIVE STAR (page 39)

Ten irregular pentagonal stars in the line pattern are shown here. Can you find any others?

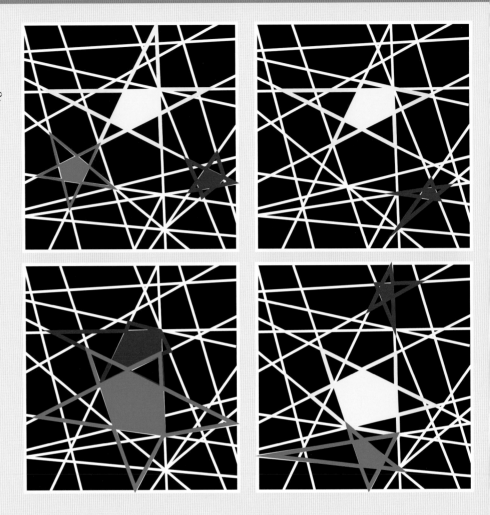

▼ DEER, OH DEER! (page 41)

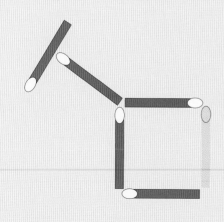

▼ DOGGED DETERMINATION (page 41)

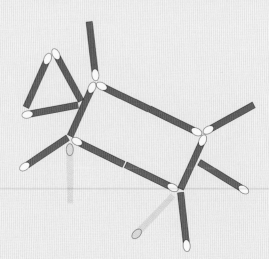

► **METAMORPHOSIS (page 42)**

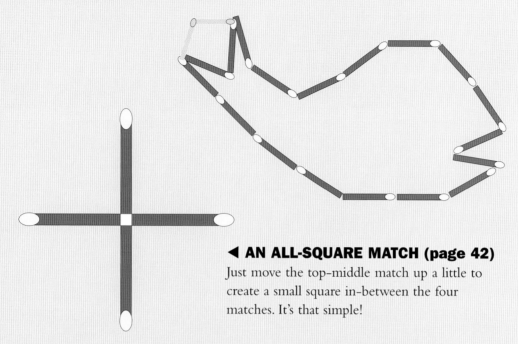

◄ **AN ALL-SQUARE MATCH (page 42)**
Just move the top–middle match up a little to create a small square in-between the four matches. It's that simple!

▼ **EVERYTHING'S EQUAL (page 43)**

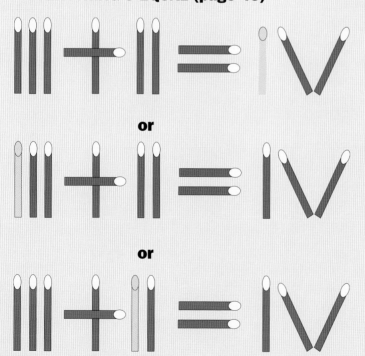

or

or

▼ **MATCH PLAY (page 43)**

▼ **ARTY-CRAFTY (pages 44–45)**

▶ **PIPE BAND (page 46)**

The band consists of four curved sections and four straight lines. The four curved sections are all $1/4$ of a circle. Since the circumference of a circle $= \pi \times$ diameter, these total $\pi \times 1 = \pi$. Each straight line $= 2d = 2$. Hence the total $= 8 + \pi$ units.

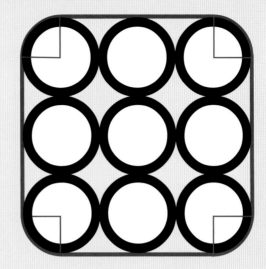

▼ **COVERT CUBES (page 47)**

There are nine skeleton rectangular prisms as shown.

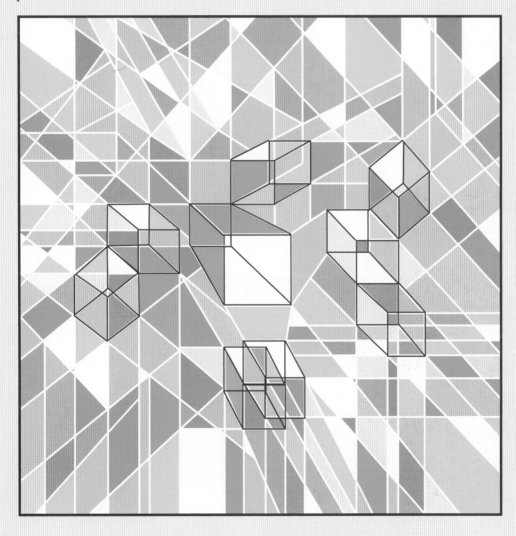

▶ TRACK AND TRACE (page 48)

The first image can be traced but only if you begin and end at the two points marked by the red dots. The second image can be traced if you start at any junction. The third image cannot be traced without lifting your pencil off the page because there are more than two places (marked with red dots) where an odd number of lines meet.

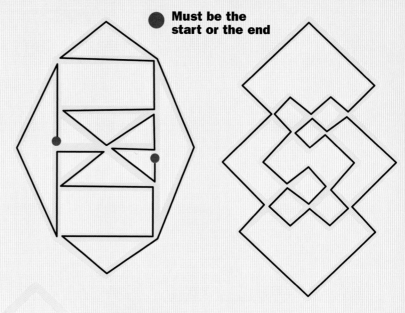

● Must be the start or the end

Impossible

▶ TRACE ELEMENTS (page 49)

It is possible to traverse the entire diagram except for one line. For example, if you begin at B and end at A, the line between C and D will not be possible to trace.

As per the previous puzzle, it is impossible to trace the entire diagram because there are four places (A, B, C, and D) where an odd number of paths meet—a network is traversable only if the number of such places is 0 or 2.

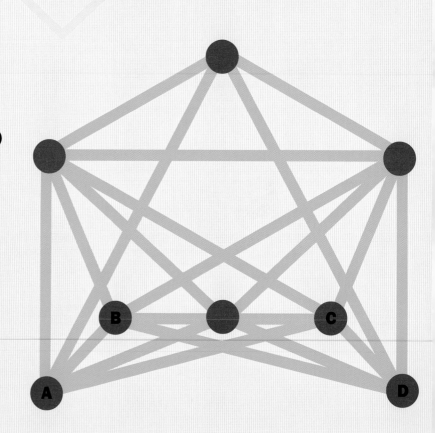

RETURN JOURNEYS
(pages 50–51)

Of the 13 different patterns, you can draw the following:

2, 3, 5, 6, 7, 9, 10, 11, 12, and 13.

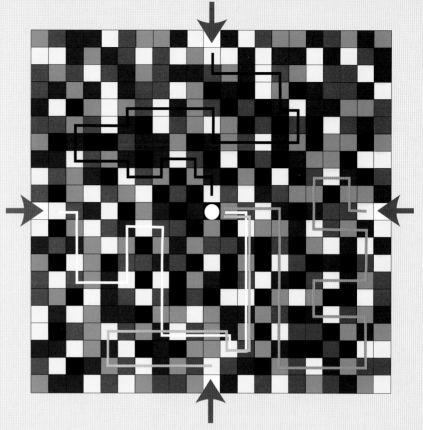

▶ FOUR-WAY MAZE (page 52)

The bottom arrow leads to the shortest path to the center.

◀ INSECT-A-SIDE (page 53)

This is one of my solutions, which visits all but two cells.

Can you do better?

THE SHOELACE PROBLEM (page 54)

The zigzag lacing uses the least lace, leaving you with the longest bow when you tie your shoe, so it's the most efficient. The straight lacing comes next, followed by the quick lacing.

If we don't have to alternate through the eyelets on the left and right sides of the shoe, even shorter lacings such as the bow tie are possible.

TOT UP A TON (page 55)

There are various solutions. We give a few here. Can you find any others?

$123 - 45 - 67 + 89 = 100$
$1 + 2 + 34 - 5 + 67 - 8 + 9 = 100$
$123 - 4 - 5 - 6 - 7 + 8 - 9 = 100$

LET IT ROLL (page 55)

Mutually exclusive events are related in such a way that only one of them can possibly happen. To discover the probability that any of them will occur, take the sum of their individual probabilities.

Rolling a four with one die is $1/6$. So this is also the chance of rolling a six.

The probability of rolling either of them on any given toss is:

$1/6 + 1/6 = 2/6 = 1/3$.

▼ HAPPY END PROBLEM (page 56)

It takes five points to guarantee a convex quadrilateral.

This was elegantly proven by the Erdös-Szekeres theorem. If you surround the given points by a rubber band (like lassoing the points), there can only be three possibilities:

1. The band forms a convex quadrilateral (with the fifth point inside);

2. The band forms a pentagon—connecting two vertices of which will always result in a convex quarilateral;

3. The band will form a triangle, with two points inside. Draw a line through the two interior points—on one side will be one vertex, on the other will be two. Take the latter two vertices and the two interior points—these will make a convex quadrilateral.

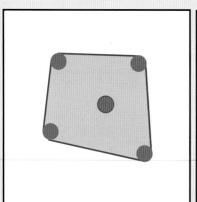
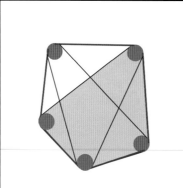
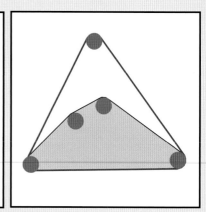

▶ EVEN HAPPIER END (page 57)

It has been proven that a convex pentagon can always be drawn in any configuration of nine randomly placed points. Eight points can be placed (as shown) without creating a convex pentagon. Any additional point will unavoidably create a convex pentagon.

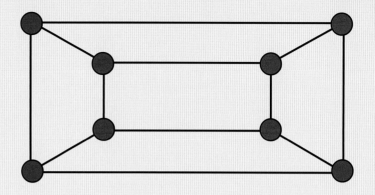

▼ LOCAL AREA NETWORK (page 59)

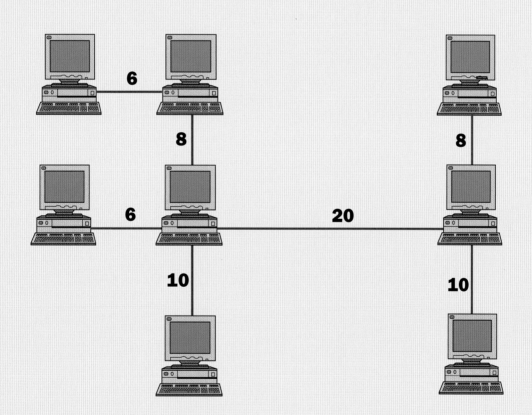

BRANCH LINES (page 59)

There would be 1,024 birds sitting on the branches of the 10th generation of a binary tree (2^{10}).

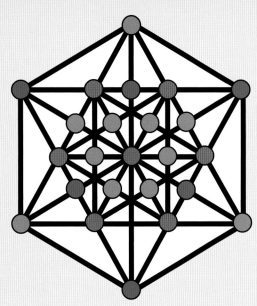

◀ TRIAL SEPARATION (page 60)

Three colors are sufficient, as shown.
(Other colorings are possible.)

▶ FISH OUT OF WATER (page 61)

Vertex coloring of the graph requires three colors as shown.

Fish with vertices of the same color can go safely into the same aquarium, of which three will be needed, as shown.

COMMUTER COMPUTATION (page 62)

You might think that you can add up the speeds and average them, like so: (28 + 56)/2 = 42, or in km (45 + 90)/2 = 67.5. Unfortunately, with speeds it isn't that simple.

No matter what the distance between home and office, the average speed is 37.28 mph (60 km/h).

To work it out, suppose that the journey to work took one hour; the return journey would naturally take two hours. Therefore I traveled 111.8 miles (180 km) in three hours, which gives the answer above.

THE GRADUATE (page 63)

Yes, and for the following reasons:

Year	Company 1	Company 2
1	5,000 + 5,300 = 10,300	10,000
2	5,600 + 5,900 = 11,500	11,200
3	6,200 + 6,500 = 12,700	12,400
4	6,800 + 7,100 = 13,900	13,600
5	7,400 + 7,700 = 15,100	14,800

Company 1's offer is $300 a year better than company 2's.

▼ SQUARE DIVISION (page 67)

Three identical squares inscribed in an equilateral triangle are shown here dissecting it into 28 regions (12 red, 12 orange, 1 yellow, and 3 pink).

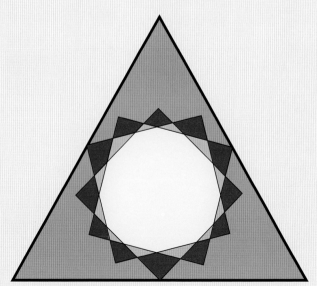

A SUITE DEAL? (page 63)

She was wrong.

$1,200 is 125% of $960 (she made a $240 profit).

$1,200 is 80% of $1,500 (her loss was $300).

The combined sale had a loss of $60.

▼ YOU ARE FEELING VERY SLEEPY... (page 66)

The red spiral occupies exactly one-sixth of the hexagon. You can divide the entire hexagon into six identical spiral arms as shown.

HERE'S THE PLAN 1 (pages 70–71)

A–4; B–2; C–1; D–4

HERE'S THE PLAN 2 (pages 72–73)

E–4; F–4; G–1; H–4

CAN I HAVE YOUR ORTHOGRAPHIC? & SOLID STATE (pages 74–77)

The corresponding answers for the puzzles on pages 74–75 are found in the puzzles on pages 76–77 and vice-versa (so 1 = 1, for example)!

▼ ART PYRAMID (page 78)

The pattern seen is a big red square.

▼ THE VIEW FROM ABOVE (page 79)

It can be either of the two views shown here. We have no indication of the height of the structure.

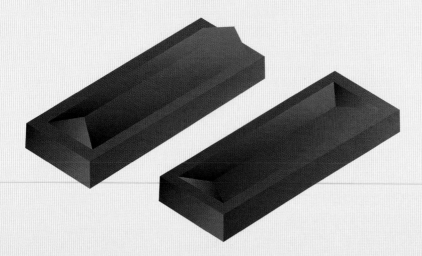

▼ HIDE AND SEEK (pages 80–81)

▼ TIM'S TURTLE (page 83)

A circle, or as near to a circle as you can get, will always maximize the space available.

ALIEN-NATION (page 83)

The first must have said "I'm an alien," for, if he is an alien, he can't tell a lie and, if he is a human being, he can't tell the truth. Therefore (2) is telling the truth and is an alien.

This results in two possible outcomes:

Alien–Alien–Human or Human–Alien–Alien

Conclusion: There are more aliens than human beings.

STATUS SYMBOLS: A QUIZ
(pages 84–85)

1. Infinity
2. Approaches (in value)
3. And so on
4. Equal to or less than
5. Equal to
6. Therefore
7. Sum of terms
8. Equal to or greater than
9. Less than
10. Square root
11. Similar to (proportional)
12. Corresponds to
13. Intersecting circles
14. Plus or minus
15. Approximately equal to
16. Identically equal to
17. Not equal to
18. Diameter
19. Circumference
20. Tangent
21. Radius
22. Sector
23. Segment
24. Scalene triangle
25. Rhombus
26. Parallelogram
27. Trapezoid
28. Kite
29. Equilateral triangle
30. Right triangle
31. Circle
32. Isosceles triangle
33. Acute angle
34. Right angle
35. Obtuse angle
36. Congruent to
37. Tetrahedron
38. Parallelepiped
39. Cube
40. Sphere
41. Cone
42. Octahedron
43. Regular pentagon
44. Regular hexagon
45. Regular heptagon
46. Regular octagon
47. Cylinder
48. Pyramid
49. Regular nonagon
50. Cuboid

▼ CLOWN AND COMPANY (pages 86–87)

Here are our suggestions, but the main thing is to have fun!

Mr. Clown   **Sister**

Mother   **Father**

▼ FOUR-POINTED STAR (page 88)

Three folds are required.

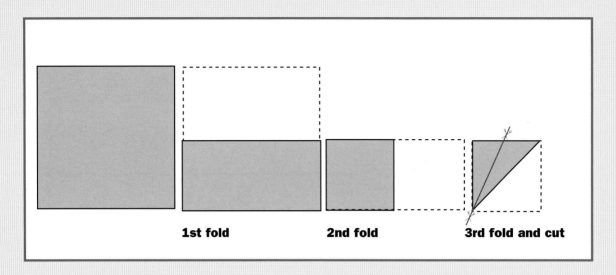

1st fold   2nd fold   3rd fold and cut

▼ SIX-POINTED STAR
(page 89)

Four folds are required.

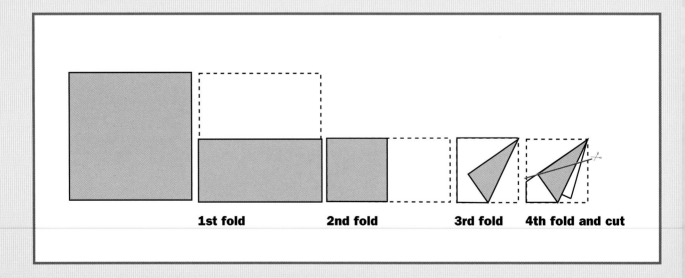

1st fold   2nd fold   3rd fold   4th fold and cut

▶ LUTHER'S PROOF (page 89)

Move the pencil via the turns shown, with each turn equaling one of the angles of the triangle. When you have finished, the pencil is pointing in the opposite direction from where it started. Therefore, it must have turned 180 degrees and that's the total of the angles in the triangle.

Other simple proofs of the same result include tearing the corners from a paper triangle and lining them up or, more elegantly, folding the corners (A, B, and C) toward the baseline (as shown).

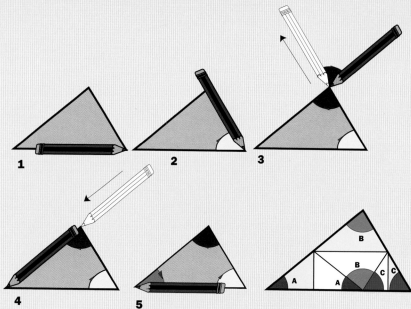

◀ SIX-SIDED SYMMETRY (page 91)

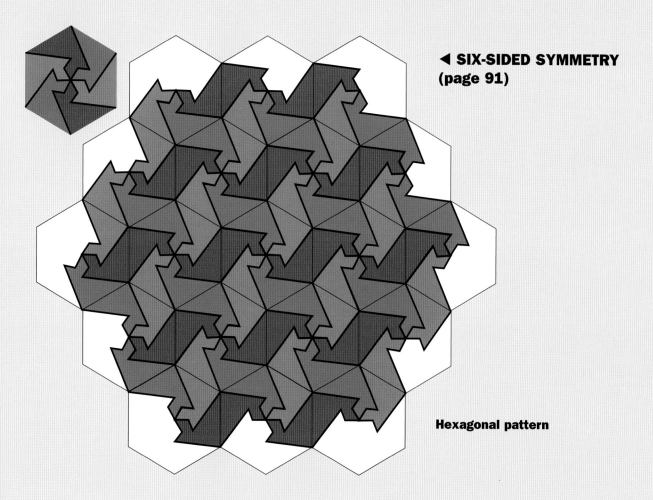

Hexagonal pattern

▶ ANAGRAM GRID
(page 92)

The grid shows a score of 26 points.
Other answers are possible.

T	M	S	D	M	N	E	I	A	R	■
T	R	I	M	■	A	M	E	N	D	S
T	R	I	M	S	■	N	A	M	E	D
D	R	E	A	M	■	M	I	N	T	S
S	M	A	R	T	■	D	E	N	I	M
M	I	N	T	E	D	■	R	A	M	S
M	I	N	D	S	E	T	■	A	R	M
T	A	N	D	E	M	■	R	I	M	S
M	A	D	M	E	N	■	S	T	I	R
D	I	M	M	E	R	S	■	A	N	T
M	A	S	T	E	R	M	I	N	D	■

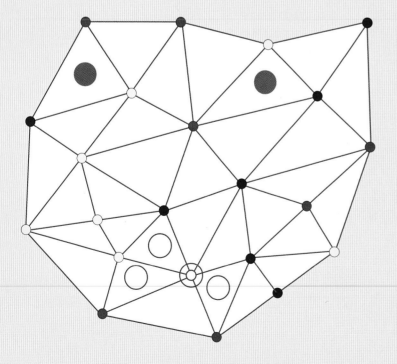

◀ THE COMPLETE ANGLER
(page 93)

At the outset, let's suppose we create two
complete triangles (indicated by the discs).
No matter how we color the remaining
dots, it seems that creating a third complete
triangle is unavoidable. In the diagram
shown, coloring the final dot red, yellow, or
blue will complete one of the triangles
marked by the white circles.

This result is known as Sperner's lemma.
It says that a polygon with an odd (or
even) number of sides leads to an odd (or
even) number of complete triangles. Since
our polygon has 11 sides, it is impossible to
create a color scheme that has only two
complete triangles.

▼ FLY THE FLAG (page 94)

Here is a complete flag.

The flag puzzle was inspired by one of the geometric designs of the famous conceptual artist Sol LeWitt.

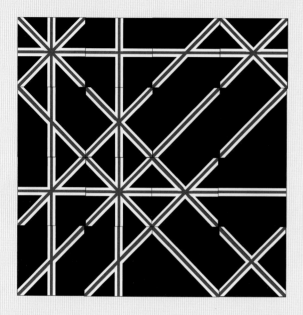

▼ FLAG THE FLY (page 95)

One of the many possible solutions is shown here.

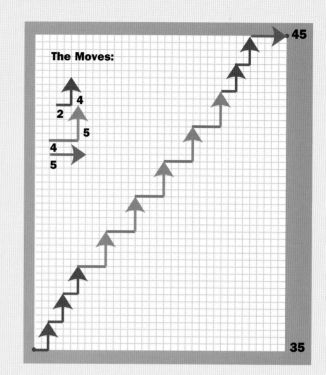

◄ AN ARROW ESCAPE (page 96)

Here we show a path that visits all but three cells.

Can you do better?

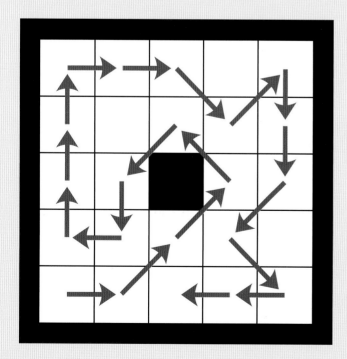

▼ AT NO POINT... (page 97)

Each cell is visited, as shown here.

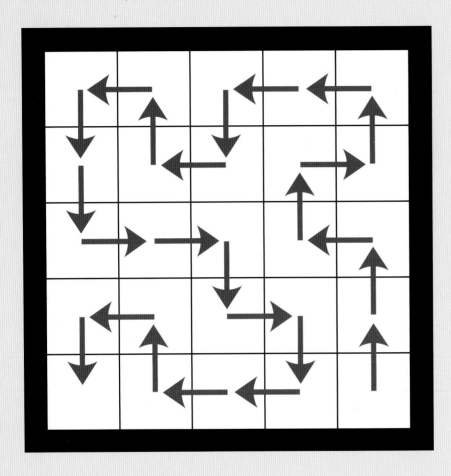